INSIGHT CO[M]

SCOTLAND

Compact Guide: Scotland is the ultimate quick-reference guide to this popular destination. It tells you all you need to know about the country's attractions, from the rural delights of the Lowlands to the rugged splendour of the Highlands and islands, from the romance of its castles and glens to the vibrant culture of its cities.

This is one of 130 Compact Guides, combining the interests and enthusiasms of two of the world's best-known information providers: Insight Guides, whose titles have set the standard for visual travel guides since 1970, and Discovery Channel, the world's premier source of nonfiction television programming.

Discovery CHANNEL

APA PUBLICATIONS
Part of the Langenscheidt Publishing Group

Insight Compact Guide: Scotland

Written by: Berndt Müller
English version by: Susan Bollans
Edited by: Maria Lord
Photography by: Bill Wassman
Additional photography by: Marcus Brooke 16/17, 32, 50/2, 51/1, 52/2,
     62/1, 71, 75/2, 78/2, 79, 85, 86, 87/1, 88, 89/1/2, 95/2, 99/2, 100, 101/1
     Jerry Dennis 28, 29/1/2, 30, 31, 33/1/2, 34, 35/1/2, 36/1/2, 37, 53
     104, 105/1
     Courtesy The Glasgow Science Centre 13
Cover picture by: Bill Wassman
Design: Graham Mitchener
Picture Editor: Hilary Genin
Maps: Dave Priestley

Editorial Director: Brian Bell
Managing Editor: Tony Halliday

CONTACTING THE EDITORS: As every effort is made to provide accurate
information in this publication, we would appreciate it if readers would
call our attention to any errors and omissions by contacting:
Apa Publications, PO Box 7910, London SE1 1WE, England.
Fax: (44 20) 7403 0290. e-mail: insight@apaguide.demon.co.uk

Information has been obtained from sources believed to be reliable,
but its accuracy and completeness, and the opinions based thereon,
are not guaranteed.

First Edition 1996
Second Edition 2002
Printed in Singapore by Insight Print Services (Pte) Ltd
Original edition © Polyglott-Verlag Dr Bolte KG, Munich

Worldwide distribution enquiries:
APA Publications GmbH & Co. Verlag KG (Singapore Branch)
38 Joo Koon Road, Singapore 628990
Tel: (65) 865-1600, Fax: (65) 861-6438

Distributed in the UK & Ireland by:
GeoCenter International Ltd
The Viables Centre, Harrow Way, Basingstoke,
Hampshire RG22 4BJ
Tel: (44 1256) 817987, Fax: (44 1256) 817-988

Distributed in the United States by:
Langenscheidt Publishers, Inc.
46–35 54th Road, Maspeth, NY 11378
Tel: (1 718) 784-0055, Fax: (1 718) 784-0640

www.insightguides.com

SCOTLAND

◁ **Edinburgh (p18)**
The country's capital has a fascinating history, some exemplary town planning and is the venue for one of Europe's largest arts festivals.

▷ **Skye (p81)**
The Black Cuillin ridge makes Skye the most dramatic of the Hebrides.

▽ **Glencoe (p97)**
A impressive glen, site of the infamous massacre.

◁ **Glasgow (p28)**
Scotland's most lively and design-conscious city has lost most of its heavy industry and is reinventing itself as a centre for science and the arts, while retaining its gritty charm.

▽ **Dunnottar Castle (p61)** A spectacular fortress perched high above the sea.

△ **Burns (p48)**
Visit the poet's resting place in Dumfries; one of many shrines to Scotland's literary heritage.

◁ **Melrose Abbey (p46)** A romantic ruin, set in the beautiful Borders region, that has inspired many artists.

▽ **Forth Rail Bridge (p55)** One of the greatest engineering achievements of the 19th century.

△ **The Whisky Trail (p63)** A tour of some of Scotland's best-loved institutions, its distilleries.

◁ **Calanais (p86)** This important and atmospheric prehistoric site is found on the Island of Lewis.

Land of Surprises

For many people Scotland is a target for jokes about haggis, stinginess and men in skirts – the country of bagpipes and whisky. Those of a less frivolous nature may associate it with beautiful, rugged scenery and the oil rigs off the North Sea coast.

Like most caricatures and generalisations, these are based on fact, but are only a small part of the picture. Some American visitors will not see a single kilted Scotsman playing the bagpipes during the whole of their Scottish holiday, only to encounter one at a function back home organised by people who have family ties with a Scottish clan. Jokes about the legendary stinginess of the Scots are so widespread that they are even exploited by the Bank of Scotland to advertise its services. But within Great Britain the Scots are known for quite different things: for example, the most unhealthy diet and (as a direct consequence) the highest rate of heart disease in the European Union. On the positive side, the crime rate is much lower than England's, and the sense of humour is anarchic.

POLITICS OF DIFFERENCE

The Scots increasingly try to sharpen the distinction between their country and England. Nothing annoys them more than the classification of the cultural achievements of their ancestors as 'English literature' or 'English architecture' – two areas, incidentally, where there is no lack of famous Scottish names. When the Englishman Henry Havelock Ellis compiled a list of 'British geniuses' in 1904, he established that from a statistical point of view the Scots were remarkably over-represented. Politically, Scotland has long been to the left of England – never more than in the 1997 general election, after which not a single Conservative MP was left in Scotland. This position had barely improved by 2001, when they regained just one seat from the Scottish Nationalists.

Thus we have a country which on the one hand has its share of social and political problems, of which continental Europe is more or less unaware,

Ancient inhabitants
Scotland has been occupied since at least 6000BC. Findings of mussel shells and stone tools indicate that there were hunters and gatherers living on the Scottish coasts at this time.

Opposite: Edinburgh Castle
Below: Crail harbour
Bottom: cycling through Torridon

and on the other conjures up a number of stock images. The surprising thing about all this is that Scotland nevertheless fulfils almost all expectations: the visitor who wants bagpipe music, kilts and whisky distilleries will find them at the Highland Games and on the 'Malt Whisky Trail' in Speyside. The lover of solitude, grandiose landscapes and relatively unspoilt nature will be equally rewarded, and those in pursuit of the cultural delights of art, architecture and the performing arts will have time for little else.

The River Dee

POSITION AND SIZE

Scotland occupies the northern third of mainland Great Britain together with the surrounding islands (the Hebrides and the Orkney and Shetland Islands). Edinburgh is at approximately the same latitude as Copenhagen and Moscow, while the northernmost tip of the Scottish mainland is level with Stockholm.

The country has a surface area of 30,394 sq miles (78,720 sq km), 34 percent of the area of Great Britain. It is divided into three geological regions: the Southern Uplands is a 50-mile (80-km) band of hills with a maximum height of just over 2,625ft (800 metres), which extends from the English border to just south of Edinburgh and Glasgow. These two cities lie in the central area known as the Lowlands, a strip of relatively flat country running from the southwest to the northeast, and the most fertile and densely populated part of Scotland.

In the north, the central Lowlands border on the Highlands, which are in turn divided by the fault known as the Great Glen (Loch Ness, Loch Lochy and Loch Linnhe): on one side are the Eastern Highlands with the Grampian Mountains, while the area to the west and north of the Great Glen is the most thinly populated part of Great Britain, with mountains up to 4,265ft (1,300 metres) in height, sparse vegetation and the oldest geological formations in Western Europe.

LANDSCAPE AND WILDLIFE

With the exception of a few inaccessible strips of coast and remote, uninhabited islands, even the wildest and most sparsely populated parts of Scotland cannot be classified as completely unspoilt. Forestry, sheep breeding and management of the land for hunting have affected the flora and fauna, even in those areas far from population centres and main roads, and the most attractive areas are now at risk due to the expansion of tourism.

The suitability of the Lowlands and Southern Uplands for farming was recognized and exploited by early settlers, but until the Highland Clearances of the late-18th and early 19th century *(see box)*, farming was predominantly on a subsistence level, with relatively little interference in local ecosystems – although people's need for wood destroyed the old Caledonian (north Scottish) forests.

In Scotland you are never very far from the sea, and the rocky coastline ranks with the ranges of almost treeless hills and mountains as the most typical natural features of Scotland. It is no wonder that some of the largest and most varied colonies of sea birds in Europe are to be found on the islands and coasts in the north and west. In addition, in certain areas attempts are being made to prevent the extinction of local species such as wild cats, otters and ospreys, which have already dwindled greatly in numbers.

The Highland Clearances

The clearance of vast tracts of northwest Scotland between 1784 and 1850 is one of the saddest chapters in the history of the Highlands. After the defeat of the third Jacobite uprising in 1746, the lands of many clan chiefs were confiscated. By the time they were restored by the government in 1784, many chiefs were living in Edinburgh or London and employed administrators to obtain maximum profits on their behalf. Sheep farming, which produced the highest returns, was introduced to the area on a massive scale. Lowland herders moved in and existing tenants were forcibly driven from their homes. By the time of the last clearances in 1853–4, the Highlands of Wester Ross and Sutherland had been almost completely depopulated. The damage caused can still be seen today in the overgrown remains of villages dotting the region.

Grazing in the Highland Wildlife Park

CLIMATE CHART

Braemar

°C J F M A M J J A S O N D mm
20
15
10
5
0
-5
160
120
80
40
0

Edinburgh

°C J F M A M J J A S O N D mm
20
15
10
5
0
160
120
80
40
0

Stornoway

°C J F M A M J J A S O N D mm
20
15
10
5
0
160
120
80
40
0

☐ Maximum temperature
■ Minimum temperature
— Rainfall
☀ Sunny months

Kilchurn Castle on Loch Awe

CLIMATE

The Scottish climate is characterised by mild Atlantic weather in the west (through the influence of the Gulf Stream), with high rainfall and relatively small variations in temperature – in winter it is less cold, but in summer less warm than the eastern North Sea Coast, where conditions are harsher but it rains far less frequently. The Edinburgh area, where it rains on average 175 days a year, has the lowest rainfall, and the Outer Hebrides the highest (around 250 days a year).

Rapid changes in the weather are the norm – stout shoes and an anorak are advised for visitors venturing outdoors for any length of time, even in summer. But 'rapid change' must not automatically be interpreted as a change for the worse.

WHEN TO GO

The best time to visit Scotland is between the middle of June and the first weeks of September, when daytime temperatures are often over 68°F (20°C). Mid-May to mid-June and the end of September/beginning of October are quieter because they do not coincide with the British school holidays, and there are also unlikely to be severe storms – in the northwest early autumn is often the pleasantest time of year. The relatively short winter sports season is at its height in January and February.

POPULATION AND RELIGION

Scotland has a population of 5.1 million, of Celtic, Anglo-Saxon and Scandinavian origin. However, in the early-21st century, even on the remote Orkney Islands, a substantial number of the 'local' people do not even speak with a Scottish accent, let alone belong to a family that has been associated with the country for generations.

Communities with such families do still exist, especially in the Outer Hebrides where a few thousand people continue to speak Gaelic, but in general immigration and exchanges of population with other parts of Great Britain have made Scotland as cosmopolitan as other European regions. Some experts nevertheless consider that one reason why the Highlands have the highest suicide rate in Britain is the breakdown of traditional social structures.

The existence of a state church may give the impression that Scotland is a purely Protestant country, but a survey showed that almost as many Scots are adherents of the Roman Catholic faith (794,000) as of the Church of Scotland (823,000).

There is a particularly high proportion of Catholics in industrial towns such as Glasgow and Dundee, which have large Irish populations, and there are also old-established Catholic communities in the Highlands and the southern islands of the Outer Hebrides.

GOVERNMENT AND POLITICS

Geographically, Scotland could be termed the northernmost province of Great Britain, but this is a description guaranteed to anger the majority of its population, who have been increasingly hostile to rule by London.

The nature of the British monarchy and the absence of a written constitution resulted in a number of contradictions: for example, Scotland had its own legal system, which differed considerably from the English one, but all laws were passed at Westminster in London.

This system of administration was upheld by successive Conservative governments, which

The Presbyterians
The Presbyterian Church, the Church of Scotland, is generally regarded as the embodiment of Scotland's national characteristics: its Calvinistic ethos places a high value on hard work and obedience to authority, but also on intellectual independence. Love of argument, pursued to the point of stubbornness, is said to be a particular characteristic of the smaller Protestant groups known as the Free Churches.

A display of national pride outside Edinburgh Castle

feared that any degree of devolution for Scotland would result in the break-up of the UK. At the other extreme, the Scottish National Party (SNP) wanted 'an independent Scotland which is part of the European Union'. The Conservatives' authority vanished after the 1997 general election, which left them without a single Scottish MP, and the incoming Labour administration rapidly organised a referendum asking the Scots two questions: did they want a devolved parliament in Edinburgh and, if so, should it have its own tax-raising powers?

Below: remains of an industrial past along the Clyde
Bottom: an exhibition of Lewis tweed

The result was decisive: 74 percent of voters said yes to the first question and 63 per cent said yes to the second. Less decisive were the results of the Scottish parliament elections held in May 1999, which saw Labour having to form a coalition administration with the Liberal Democrats.

When the first Scottish parliament for 300 years opened in 1999, there were of course also seats for the SNP, who see the parliament as a stepping stone towards their ultimate goal of independence for Scotland. The 2001 general election saw little change in the political map of Scotland, with no sign of a substantial increase in support for the nationalists (who lost one seat to the Tories).

ECONOMY AND ENVIRONMENT

The Scottish economy depends for its survival on two industries: tourism and North Sea oil. Tourism and the related industries (crafts, etc) provide work for far more people than any other branch of the economy (the Scottish Tourist Board has estimated tourist spending in Scotland to be £2.2 billion a year), while oil produces enormous tax revenues, and large profits for successful businesses.

But neither are without their problems. Areas attractive to tourists are in danger of being spoiled by too many visitors, and work in the service industries is often badly paid and carried out by unqualified people. Drilling for oil (and gas) off the North Sea coast is a crisis-prone undertaking, most of the tax goes straight to London, and only a few of the successful enterprises are in Scottish hands.

SCIENCE AND INDUSTRY

The heavy industries for which Scotland was once famous have almost completely disappeared – in the past 10 years the last but one of the large shipyards, the last steelworks and the last large colliery in Scotland have closed down. Hopes for the industrial sector are now pinned on the development of high-tech firms.

The 1980s were supposed to mark the establishment of a 'Silicon Glen' between Edinburgh and Glasgow, where more computer components are produced than anywhere else in Europe. While Scotland has made important breakthroughs in the fields of biotechnology and genetics – in 1997, for example, Scottish scientists succeeded in cloning a sheep from DNA taken from cells in an adult sheep's udder – more solid, if more modest, prospects are provided by export-oriented trades and industries. Some of these already have a long tradition in Scotland: food-processing (cakes, preserves), textiles (knitwear and tweed), whisky and fish-farming (in particular salmon).

Opinion is divided over the question of industrial development *(see box)*: some people welcome the prospect of a regular source of income without having to leave their home region, while others not only deplore the damage done to the environment, but see it as a threat to their livelihood from the tourist trade, livestock or fishing.

Super quarries
The conflict between conserving the environment and providing jobs is particularly acute in the poorest parts of Scotland. For example, there have been plans to start 'super quarries' in the midst of the most beautiful landscape on the west coast, where mountains would be levelled to provide metal for road-building. In Glensanda, north of Oban, one quarry is already in operation, but numerous objections have delayed the approval of the others.

The Glasgow Science Centre

HISTORICAL HIGHLIGHTS

***circa* 4000BC** The first signs of settlement (houses built on stilts). Burial cairns and standing stones are typical of the transition from the Stone Age to the Bronze Age. Numerous finds in the Orkneys and Hebrides indicate that the islands in the north and west were heavily populated in the Stone and Bronze Ages.

800BC Immigration of Celtic tribes from Gallia to the British Isles. They are later given the name of Picts (the painted ones) by Romans settlers in the far north.

***circa* AD82 onwards** The Roman Emperor Vespasian tries to subjugate the Picts; in the area north of Dundee (Mons Graupius) the legions of Agricola defeat an army of Picts led by Calgacus, whom Tacitus credits with saying of the Romans that 'They create barren wastes and call it peace'. The Picts withdraw to the Highlands and develop effective guerilla tactics. All attempts to bring peace to the region fail, including those of Emperor Severus in 208. The Romans resort to building fortifications along the border (Hadrian's Wall).

***circa* 3rd century** The Celtic Scots (from whom the name Scotland is derived), emigrate to Scotland from Ireland, introducing the Gaelic language and the clan system. The first Christian missionaries venture into the country from the south, but the Celtic religion, based on natural phenomena, remains dominant.

563 The conversion of Scotland to Christianity begins with the arrival of the Irish monk Columba, who establishes a community of monks on Iona.

***circa* 800** Normans, Danes and Varangians invade Scotland (in 795 the monastery of Iona is attacked). After the first wave of Viking sea raids, Norwegian jarls begin to settle in the north and become assimilated: the Viking prince Thorfinn, ruler of large parts of the northwestern mainland as well as the Orkney and Shetland Islands around 1050, grew up at the court of the Scottish King Malcolm II.

843 The Scottish Prince Kenneth Mac-Alpin forms an alliance with the Picts against the Vikings and becomes the first Scottish king.

1165 William the Lion is the Scottish monarch. His kingdom encompasses almost the whole of present-day Scotland.

After 1200 A long period of dispute over succession. English King Edward I tries to exploit the situation, but faces two opponents who become Scottish heroes: William Wallace defeats Edward in 1297 at Stirling Bridge, but is beaten at Falkirk in 1298. In 1306 Robert Bruce is crowned King of Scotland but is forced to flee from Edward. After Edward's death Bruce returns to power and defeats the English at the Battle of Bannockburn in 1314. Bruce's grandson Robert the Steward is crowned in 1371, dynastic stability is re-established. The royal house, later named Stuart, rules continuously until early in the 17th century.

1350–62 Scotland is ravaged twice by the Black Death.

15th century Founding of the first universities in Scotland – St Andrews, Glasgow (1451) and Aberdeen (1495).

1520 onwards The first Lutheran tracts are brought in by merchants. Catholic Church faces increasing pressure, especially when Henry VIII of England tries to wed his son Edward to Mary Stuart, a child of two ('The Rough Wooing'). Scottish royal family turns to France for support, but the population reacts negatively to the presence of French troops. Spokesman of the resistance is the Calvinist John Knox, who stirs up considerable public feeling against 'papism'.

1560 The 'Reformation Parliament' officially abolishes the Catholic state church.

1561 Mary Stuart ascends the throne, but is obliged to abdicate in 1567 in favour of her one-year-old son, James VI.

1603 James VI becomes James I of England, and with the personal Union of the Crowns the Stuarts rule Scotland and England for more than 100 years – interrupted in 1649–60 by the English civil war and the rule of Oliver Cromwell.

1707 After influential members of the Scottish Parliament and the Church have been persuaded with gifts of money and privileges, the 'Articles of Union', the Union of the Parliaments of England and Scotland, are ratified: the United Kingdom of Great Britain comes into being.

1714–19 Followers of the House of Stuart try to establish the claims of the son of James VII/II to the throne against George I of Hanover, crowned in 1714. The first uprising, mainly involving Highland clans under the leadership of the Earl of Mar, fails when the loyal Duke of Argyll in the Lowlands sends an army to fight the rebels. The second attempt in 1719 is crushed at the outset.

1745–6 With help from France the third Jacobite uprising, led by 'Bonnie Prince Charlie', grandson of James VII, is initially successful. However, he gains little support from the rich Lowlands, and is defeated at the battle of Culloden.

circa **1750 onwards** The advent of the industrial revolution, Scotland's economy takes off (steam engines, the textile and iron industries, shipbuilding, coal mining, overseas trade). The 'Scottish Enlightenment' produces great artists, engineers and philosophers (e.g. James Watt, Thomas Telford and David Hume). The Highland clans, tartans and bagpipes are invested with a romantic aura, but people are evicted forcibly from most of the northwest (the 'Highland Clearances').

1820 As the textile industry puts weavers out of work, the workers riot ('The Radical Wars') and are brutally suppressed; working hours and conditions are not regulated until 1877.

After 1945 Scotland's war industries switch to the production of consumer goods. With the post-war economic boom, regional issues throughout Great Britain take a back seat.

1975 The commercial extraction of oil starts off the east coast of Scotland.

1979 Partial political autonomy rejected in a referendum. Margaret Thatcher is elected and makes it clear that any form of home rule is out of the question.

1996 Stone of Destiny transferred from Westminster Abbey to Edinburgh Castle.

1997 The general election leaves the Tories without a single Scottish MP. In a referendum, 74 percent of voters opt for a separate Scottish parliament.

1999 First elections to the Scottish parliament are held on 6 May. Labour is the biggest party but is nine seats short of an overall majority, and forms a coalition with the Liberal Democrats. The late Donald Dewar becomes First Minister. The Scottish parliament opens on 1 July.

2001 Labour retain their grip on power in the general election, the Tories regain one seat from the SNP.

Map on pages 20–21

Old and new
The 18th-century town planners divided the town neatly into the primarily neoclassical New Town, and the Old Town, with its narrow winding streets. The castle, perched on top of its precipitous hill above the city, gives Edinburgh its unmistakable skyline.

*Preceding pages:
Eilean Donan castle
Below: the Scott Memorial*

1: Edinburgh

After London, Edinburgh attracts more visitors than any other city in Great Britain. The castle is the most frequently visited British tourist attraction outside London. As these two statistics indicate, Edinburgh is the alternative British metropolis, countering the overwhelming political and cultural influence of London. The city is also equipped to accommodate far more guests than its size would seem to merit: during the internationally famous festival in August the streets of the inner city are packed with people, and all available beds are reserved months in advance.

While this may make Edinburgh sound rather daunting, nothing could be further from the truth. One of the most architecturally uniform (and beautiful) cities in Europe, it is a welcoming place where visitors can spend time just soaking up the atmosphere, as well as enjoying the many historical and cultural sights.

HISTORY

The hill, called Castle Rock, is known to have been settled since the Bronze Age. When it was taken by the Angles in 638BC, King Edwin chose it for the site of his castle. One suggested origin of the name Edinburgh is that it is a derivation of 'Edwin's Burgh'.

The capital of Scotland was transferred here from Dunfermline by King David I, and with the founding of the Abbey of Holyrood in 1128, the town grew between the Castle and the monastery, in what is today known as the Royal Mile.

Edinburgh rose to prosperity in the second half of the 15th century: the first city wall, built in 1450, had to be replaced in 1513 by a second boundary, due to the town's expansion. In 1561 Edinburgh became the seat of Mary Stuart's government, and her successors continued to rule from here until 1603, when her son James VI of Scotland became James I of England as a result of the Union of the Crowns, and moved his residence and hence the centre of power to London.

EDINBURGH'S RENAISSANCE

In the latter half of the 18th century, Edinburgh's second period of prosperity began with a flurry of building activity – in 1767, in order to ease the pressure on the cramped Old Town, the architect James Craig was commissioned to design the New Town north of the castle. The generously proportioned district has been carefully preserved in its original form.

When King George IV paid a ceremonial visit to Edinburgh in 1822, the first monarch to do so for more than 100 years, he acknowledged the importance of the city as the historic centre of the 'Scottish Enlightenment', domain of the intellectual elite and seat of the judiciary and administration. But it took until 1999 before real power was returned to Edinburgh – and Scotland – when the first Scottish parliament in 300 years was opened in the city.

SIGHTS

★★ **Edinburgh Castle** , with its bird's-eye view of the surrounding streets, is a good place to get your bearings before setting out on a walk through the city. The impressive complex itself also has much to offer. Within its walls is the oldest building in the city, St Margaret's Chapel, built between 1070 and 1090, and the apartments

Star Attraction
● **Edinburgh Castle**

Below: a castle exhibit
Bottom: the view
from Calton Hill

of Mary Stuart and other sections of the complex are also open to the public. In the Crown Room are the Honours of Scotland: the sceptre, crown and sword dating from the 15th–16th centuries symbolise the independence of Scotland, which is why a clause was added to the Act of Union of 1707, when the parliaments of England and Scotland were united, to the effect that the insignia could never be removed from Scotland. The Stone of Destiny, returned to Scotland in 1996 after more than 600 years, has joined the Honours of Scotland.

Treasure hunt
The crown jewels (regalia) of Scotland were lost between 1707 and 1818, until a commission, led by Walter Scott, traced them to a locked chest within a locked room in the castle.

Within the castle complex, British military history is commemorated with the Scottish National War Memorial and the United Services Museum. The castle's forecourt, the Castle Esplanade, is the setting of the **Edinburgh Military Tattoo**, held every summer, when the Scottish regiments parade in full regalia to the music of the bagpipes.

Only a few paces from the entrance to the castle is the **Scotch Whisky Heritage Centre,** where, riding in a kind of hollowed-out whisky vat, visitors are guided through the history of the Scottish national drink.

Map below

Below: the national drink
Bottom: castle guard

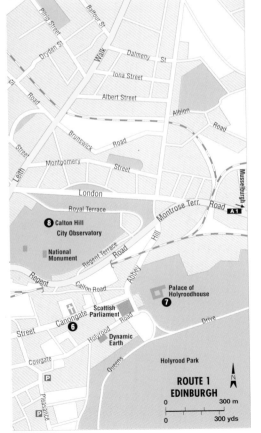

ROUTE 1
EDINBURGH
0   300 m
0   300 yds

Map
on pages
20–21

Camera Obscura
On the corner opposite Ramsay Gardens is the Outlook Tower, with the Camera Obscura on the roof. The building dates from the 17th century, and the first Camera Obscura was installed in 1853. With the superior instrument in operation today it is still a fascinating experience – for example, it's the only way the neo-Gothic stonemasonry 230ft (70m) up on the Tolbooth Church can be admired close up.

Below: street signs
Bottom: Gladstone's Land

THE ROYAL MILE

From the steep approach to the castle there is a good view over the ★ **Royal Mile** (divided into Castlehill, Lawnmarket, High Street and Canongate). From here to Holyroodhouse it is almost exactly a mile (1.5km).

Castlehill ❷ has numerous unusual buildings. Below the Whisky Centre is Cannonball House – with a cannonball embedded in the west gable, said to have been fired from the Castle during one of the many sieges. At the beginning of Ramsay Lane is Ramsay Gardens, a residential house dating from 1894, built by the eccentric Patrick Geddes and marking the start of the much-needed Old Town renovation – by the end of the 19th century the quarter had completely degenerated.

BACK STREETS

Where Castlehill joins the **Lawnmarket ❸** is the first of the small side streets, enclosed courtyards and cul-de-sacs typical of the Old Town: Milne's Court and James Court. When the present complex was built in 1700, it was one of the most desirable addresses in Edinburgh.

One building between James Court and Lawnmarket, however, is a hundred years older: **Gladstone's Land** ('land' in Scots dialect is a house for several families) has been restored as an elegant 17th-century town house and is open to the public. Next door in Lady Stair's Close, **Lady Stair's House**, from the same period, houses a museum full of memorabilia relating to Robert Burns, Walter Scott and Robert Louis Stevenson.

There is a connection between Robert Louis Stevenson and Brodie's Close opposite: it is named after Deacon Brodie, hanged in 1788, who was a highly respected town councillor by day and a burglar by night – said to have been the inspiration for Stevenson's novel *Dr Jekyll and Mr Hyde*.

THE NATIONAL MUSEUM

To the south, near the university and National Library, on Chambers Street, is the ★ **Royal**

Museum, housed in a fine Victorian building and containing a superb natural history collection. Next door is the imposing sandstone-clad ★★ **Museum of Scotland ❹**, telling the history of Scotland, completed in 1998 to bring under one roof some of Scotland's most valuable national treasures.

Star Attraction
● **Museum of Scotland**

ST GILES KIRK

From the Lawnmarket, the impressive ★ **High Kirk of St Giles**, with its crowned tower, is visible jutting out into the **High Street ❺**. The exterior – with the exception of the tower – dates from the 19th century, and only the interior gives an idea of how far back the building really goes; the oldest parts of it date from the 14th century, when it was built on the site of an even earlier, Norman church. The early-20th century **Thistle Chapel** is particularly ornate. St Giles stands on the only piece of flat ground between the Castle and Holyroodhouse: Parliament Square.

The inside of Parliament House on the south side of the square, in particular the Great Hall, is also worth seeing.

On the other side of the major junction with the main road, North Bridge/South Bridge, is the Scandic Crown Hotel, a modern concrete building with a facade designed to blend in with the surrounding houses. Diagonally opposite in

Below: the Thistle Chapel ceiling
Bottom: High Kirk of St Giles

Map
on pages
20–21

Hilltop folly
A particularly fine view of the city can be obtained from ★ **Calton Hill ⑧**. On top of this hill is a collection of unusual buildings: the Nelson Monument, which can be climbed, the City Observatory, only accessible by appointment, and the National Monument, which was never completed. Its proud creators, who built it as a memorial to fallen soldiers, intended it to outlast and become even more famous than the Parthenon of Athens on which it was modelled. Unfortunately, in 1829 they ran out of money.

Chalmer's Close is Trinity College Church, which is built with old materials, but is no more 'genuine' than the Scandic Crown. The original 15th-century building which stood down in the valley was demolished in 1848 to make way for railway lines, and 25 years later rebuilt (although never fully completed) at its present location.

JOHN KNOX'S HOUSE

Close by is a 16th-century house which, although it looks as unreal as a film set, has in fact changed hardly at all in the course of its history. **John Knox's House** is today a museum dedicated to the memory of the reformer and preacher who is said to have lived there (although all that is certain is that it belonged to a man by the not uncommon name of Knox).

Take either of the streets opposite (Hyndford Close or Fountain Close) to the **Museum of Childhood**, full of dolls and other toys, which possibly has more appeal for nostalgic adults than for today's children.

CANONGATE

The next junction marks the start of **Canongate ⑥**. Two interesting museums are located in this section of the Royal Mile: first, the **People's Story Museum** in the picturesque building that was once the court prison, Canongate Tollbooth. Here, the social history of Edinburgh is reconstructed from the standpoint of the working population, by means of authentically furnished rooms, photographs and everyday objects.

Huntly House, on the other side of the road, provides an insight into the history of the city, with prehistoric, Roman and Celtic finds, craft objects and portraits. A passage next to Huntly House leads into one of the best-preserved courtyards in the city, **Bakehouse Close**. Some of the closes leading off Canongate are well worth investigating: tucked away in Lochend Close, for example, is Panmure House, where the economist Adam Smith lived until his death in 1790.

John Knox

HOLYROOD

★★ **Holyroodhouse** ❼, at the bottom end of
Canongate, is the official Scottish residence of
the Queen. The palace was originally the Abbey
guesthouse, and the present building was completed around 1671. The areas open to the public are the State Apartments, the Picture Gallery
and the Historic Apartments of Mary Stuart.
Holyroodhouse is about to be overlooked by a
new **Scottish Parliament** building, currently
under construction on the left-hand side facing
the palace. Directly opposite the parliament site,
across Holyrood Road in a spectacular setting
beneath the Salisbury Crags, is a new visitor
attraction, ★★ **Dynamic Earth**, incorporating displays on the formation and evolution of the planet.

Star Attractions
● **Holyroodhouse**
● **Dynamic Earth**

Below: Holyrood interior
Bottom: Holyroodhouse

PRINCES STREET

Walk down Calton Hill along Waterloo Place and
past the main station into ★ **Princes Street** ❾. On
the right the shop fronts spoil the effect of the
Georgian architecture, but this is compensated for
by the park on the left, with the **Scott Monument**
and the precipitous Castle Rock as a backdrop.
When James Craig designed the New Town, he
created three long axes (with George Street in the
middle), leaving the outer sides open (to the north
of Queen Street and the south of Princes Street).

Map on pages 20–21

Where Princes Street is joined by The Mound there is a spacious square, the location of the **Royal Scottish Academy** of art, sculpture and architecture and the ★★ **National Gallery of Scotland** ❿. The National Gallery dates from the mid-19th century, and has been extended considerably. The collection of paintings is one of the most important in Europe, and it includes major works by Scottish artists *(see page 103).*

CHARLOTTE SQUARE

Parallel to Princes Street is George Street, at the eastern end of which is ★★ **Charlotte Square** ⓫. Designed in 1791 by Robert Adam, this is a masterpiece of Scottish neoclassical architecture. The **Georgian House**, no.7, has been furnished in period style and is open to the public.

To the north of Charlotte Square is Queen Street, with the ★ **National Portrait Gallery** at the far end. Beyond lies the 19th-century extension of the New Town, with its elegant squares and residences. Moray Place and the Royal Circus are especially worth a visit; the design and architecture of these two circles of houses reflect the status of their original owners.

After crossing the **Water of Leith**, the city's main river (with an attractive riverside path), there is no better place to end an exploration of Edin-

Below: Water of Leith footpath
Bottom: Charlotte Square

burgh than the ★ **Royal Botanic Gardens** ⑫. They not only contain one of the major botanical collections in the world (including magnificent rhododendrons) but they are also a place where people go to relax – the lawns are there to be walked on. In addition to the famous Victorian Palm House, another building in the park which is worth a look at is Inverleith House, a Georgian country mansion dating from 1774, which is now used for exhibitions. The Botanic Gardens Cafeteria near the house has good food and a wonderful view from the tables outside.

Star Attractions
● National Gallery of Scotland
● Charlotte Square
● National Gallery of Modern Art

WEST END ATTRACTIONS

The ★★ **Scottish National Gallery of Modern Art** lies to the west of the city centre in Belford Road, and has a superb collection of major 20th-century works by artists such as Picasso, Matisse and Vuillard, German expressionists and Scottish colourists. Across the road is the **Dean Gallery** with more magnificent works.

★ **Edinburgh Zoo** is also located to the west (Corstorphine Road/A8, open daily from 9am) and the animals are successfully kept in natural surroundings (it includes a famous penguin pool). With its child-oriented approach, it is extremely popular amongst families, even though the ethics of keeping animals in zoos are being questioned.

> **Creepy crawlies**
> A recommended attraction is the ★ **Butterfly and Insect World** off the A7 south of the city (bus connection), with hundreds of the most unusual and colourful butterflies from all around the world (daily, summer, 9.30am–5.30pm, winter, 10am–5pm, closed Christmas Day and New Year).

Scottish National Gallery of Modern Art

LEITH

Leith, Edinburgh's harbour to the northeast of the city, has a picturesque atmosphere which is all its own. Following the decline of merchant shipping, the village, in particular the harbour quarter, went through a long period of unemployment and neglect, but has now re-emerged as a fashionable area. The street known as Shore, on the banks of the Water of Leith where it flows into the harbour, has a number of inviting restaurants and pubs, while on the other side of the river is the Customs House, an interesting building dating from the early 19th century. The Scottish Executive is housed in new buildings here.

Map
on pages
30–31

Cultural centre
In 1990 Glasgow was chosen as European Cultural Capital, and in 1999 it became UK City of Architecture and Design. While there are no overall architectural characteristics, the city does have some of the most important art nouveau buildings in Europe (Glasgow style), magnificent architecture from the Victorian economic boom years, and some fine modern architecture (including the Italian Centre and Princes Square shopping meccas). Glasgow also has several museums of international repute.

George Square by night

2: Glasgow

'Edinburgh is Scottish, Glasgow is cosmopolitan,' wrote author H.V. Morton in the 1920s, and the distinction is still valid today. Until well into the 20th century, Glasgow was not only the harbour from which Scots set sail to make new lives in other lands, it was also the entry point for numerous immigrants from Ireland, Italy, India and Pakistan. Unlike Edinburgh, Glasgow was never able to pride itself on a glorious past, and the vitality for which it is famed was often paid for with social revolution and economic crises.

In recent years Glasgow has made enormous efforts to improve its image, particularly by investing in cultural events and venues. And then there are the people: in the words of the journalist Ian Nairn in 1960, 'Glasgow is without a doubt the friendliest city in Britain...' a fact which continues to delight its visitors.

HISTORY

The first church in Glasgow was built in the 6th century on the site of the present cathedral. It formed part of a monastery founded by St Mungo (also called Kentigern), the patron saint of the city, which became the centre of a steadily growing settlement. In 1175 *Glas cau* (the green place) was granted market rights by William the Lion and developed into an important trading centre. In 1451 it acquired a university (the second oldest in Scotland), but Glasgow was still small, and its religious and academic institutions were more important than the town itself. It features scarcely at all in the history of Scotland's rulers, except as the place where Mary Stuart lost her last battle (in Langside) in 1568. Medieval castles or aristocratic palaces are conspicuous by their absence.

THE INDUSTRIAL REVOLUTION

From 1700 onwards, through the combination of a natural harbour and the requirements of the new heavy industries, Glasgow's economy began to grow. Maritime trade with America (in particular tobacco and cotton) created a need for shipbuilding, which was revolutionised by iron, steel and coal-fuelled steam engines. By 1913, the shipyards on the Clyde were making almost a third of the world's steamships. The necessary labour came from the Highlands and Ireland: in 1780 Glasgow was a city with a population of 43,000; by 1861 it was almost 10 times this size (396,000), and in 1901 it had 762,000 inhabitants – approximately the same number as it has today.

Below: the 'Armadillo' at the Scottish Exhibition Centre
Bottom: West End tenements

Every economic crisis during the 19th century brought an increase in the number of people living in the notorious slums. Although one of the richest cities in the British Empire, it was also the one with the most acute social problems. The pompous Victorian architecture and the cramped estates of terraced houses, built at the same time, reflect this dichotomy.

THE MODERN CITY

The decline of heavy industry in Britain since the end of the 1960s hit Glasgow particularly hard, and it is only more recently that the negative image of drunkenness and unemployment has begun to fade, as a result of the wide range of regenerative measures and cultural activities introduced by the city council.

Map below

SIGHTS

To understand what Glasgow was like in its Victorian heyday, begin your tour on ★ **George Square ❶**. The layout of this spacious square is typically Victorian, with an interesting selection of statues and monuments. The east side of the square is taken up by the monumental town hall, the City Chambers, designed by the architect William Young in 1883–8 to the plan of a Roman Renaissance church, with facades modelled variously on Venetian and Roman styles. If you are impressed by the outside, take a look in the entrance hall, which Young called the Loggia; it shows he didn't believe in half-measures.

GLASGOW SHOPPING

★ **Buchanan Street ❷**, a pedestrian precinct, is Glasgow's finest shopping street. In addition to Frasers department store and the Highland House of Lawrie, the famous supplier of traditional Scottish dress, the Princes Square shopping centre has the most elegant and fashionable shops in the city. At the southern end of this road is Argyll Arcade, with its numerous jewellers, and on the other side of Argyle Street is the shopping centre on St Enoch Square, with a wide range of interesting shops and cafés.

Walk down from St Enoch Square towards the Clyde, and take the footbridge on the left to cross

ROUTE 2 GLASGOW

0   500 m

0   500 yds

The great and good
A fair sprinkling of Scotland's most famous names are represented by the sculptures in George Square. In addition to the dominant figure of Sir Walter Scott on his 79-ft (24-metre) column, there are (among others) statues of the chemist Thomas Graham, the publisher Thomas Campbell, politicians Robert Peel, William Gladstone and James Oswald, Lord Clyde, a general, and the engineer James Watt (all erected in the 19th century). And, of course, there is the inevitable Queen Victoria and Prince Albert.

Opposite: a Princes Square café
Below: shoppers in Buchanan Street

Map
on pages
30–31

Radical city

As a centre of heavy industry, shipping and grinding poverty, Glasgow unsurprisingly has long been a hotbed of radical politics. This tradition finds its expression today in Glasgow MSP (Member of the Scottish Parliament) Tommy Sheridan. A local hero for his battle (and imprisonment) against the 1980s Poll Tax, he now represents the Scottish Socialist Party on Glasgow City Council and in the national parliament.

over to the riverside path, which leads past the former fish market, an imposing building dating from 1873, with colonnaded doorways, which is now full of shops and stalls.

THE PEOPLE'S PALACE

This route leads to **Glasgow Green ❸**. In the 18th century this park was used for grazing, and was also the place where the cotton dyers habitually spread their material out to dry; the present park was laid out in 1815.

At the centre of the park is the delightful museum known as the **People's Palace.** Built in 1893–8 'for the recreation and education of the population of Glasgow's East End', it now houses collections and exhibitions documenting the social history of the city, which is also the theme of the large mural painted by Ken Currie.

Here, the spirit of Glasgow comes alive: exhibits inside covering the battle for female suffrage and equality, the workers' movement, daily life during the two world wars, the Glasgow Style, Victoriana, the punk movement, and much more besides, show how the city has became what it is today. The huge conservatory made of cast iron and glass adjoining the back of the People's Palace contains not only tropical plants, but also a tea room and a stage.

The People's Palace

THE BARRAS

North of the park, the area between London Road and Gallowgate is transformed every weekend indoors and out by the largest ★ **fleamarket** (known as the 'barras') in Scotland, a Glasgow institution and a great experience. On Saturday and Sunday the barrows spread out over the whole district, which swarms with tourists, local bargain-hunters and characters who may or may not be as genuine as they look. In the same area (mainly in the streets behind Bridgegate) is Paddy's Market, held from Monday to Saturday, and primarily used by the poorer sections of the population as a way of making a bit of cash.

THE NECROPOLIS

The ★★ **Cathedral Church of St Mungo** ❹ is the official name of Glasgow Cathedral, uphill from the northern end of High Street. With its impressive exterior, this 13th-century Gothic building is the most important Scottish church from this period. In the crypt are fragments of even older churches. Opposite the cathedral is the **St Mungo Museum of Religious Life**, which opened, surrounded by controversy, in 1993. It is a carefully balanced presentation of the history and practice of the six largest world religions.

The **Necropolis** ❺, on the hill behind the cathedral (modelled on the Paris cemetery, Père Lachaise), is an untidy jumble of Victorian monuments with a romantic view of the city, framed by obelisks and angels of death.

Provand's Lordship ❻ opposite the church, built for a priest in 1471, is today a museum documenting the history of Glasgow.

CHARLES RENNIE MACKINTOSH

The first stretch of Sauchiehall Street would be a perfectly ordinary pedestrian precinct with department stores if it were not for the 'Room de Luxe', the **Willow Tea Rooms** at No.217, which have been recreated on the first floor of Henderson's Gift Shop. Decorated throughout

Star Attraction
● Cathedral of St Mungo

Below: the Cathedral Church of St Mungo
Bottom: the Willow Tea Rooms

The Glasgow Style
It can be hard to escape from the art nouveau designs of Charles Rennie Mackintosh – dubbed the 'Glasgow Style' – when visiting the city. Mackintosh, who was born in 1868, was one of the foremost art nouveau architects and designers in Europe. In an at times vulgar attempt to cash in on his popularity, the city now enthusiastically markets everything from Mackintosh tea towels and T-shirts to Mackintosh jewellery.

A Glasgow School of Art sign

in lilac and silver, the interior has affinities with the 'Glasgow Style' (*see box*).

On the left-hand side of Dalhousie Street, downhill from Sauchiehall Street, is the ★★ **Glasgow School of Art ❼**, Mackintosh's greatest achievement. The older side of the building, the east side, is reminiscent of the massive architecture of Scottish castles, while the long facade with its main entrance in Renfrew Street is less severe, and the west wing, with its vertical window niches, designed in 1907 (10 years after the east side), looks positively modern. Mackintosh acknowledged that he enjoyed designing the interiors of buildings more than the exteriors, and the superb library is evidence of his genius. The building is still being used as it was intended, as an art academy, and it is not always possible to visit the rooms and the collection of sketches and watercolours without an appointment. The times of guided tours can be obtained from the Tourist Information Centre (*see page 119*).

Information on the Glasgow Style of Mackintosh can also be obtained from the Charles Rennie Mackintosh Society in Queen's Cross Church (Garscube Rd), which Mackintosh also designed.

THE WEST END

Sauchiehall Street runs right through the inner city. To the north on the other side of the urban motorway is **Kelvingrove Park ❽** and the impressive 19th-century residential complex consisting of Park Gate, Park Circus, Park Terrace and Park Quadrant. It is primarily the work of Charles Wilson (1854), with individual buildings designed by other famous architects of the time.

This was where the most influential families of Glasgow lived, and on the southern edge of the park they built their temple to the arts, the ★★ **Glasgow Art Gallery and Museum**. Its collections are as fine as any in the national museums of Edinburgh: in addition to world-famous works by artists from Botticelli to Dalí there's an excellent selection of works by 19th-century Scottish artists – most of the avant-gardists amongst them lived and worked in Glasgow. The museum would not, of course, be complete without a room devoted to the work of Charles Rennie Mackintosh.

Also well worth a visit is the ★ **Museum of Transport** in Argyle Street, opposite the Art Museum in Kelvingrove Park, with attractively displayed cars, trams, bicycles and so on, and a whole room full of model ships.

Star Attractions
● **Glasgow School of Art**
● **Glasgow Art Gallery and Museum**

Below: the University
Bottom: Hunterian Art Gallery

THE UNIVERSITY

But this is by no means the final example of the Glasgow Style: north of the museum, to the left of Kelvin Way, the broad footpath through the park, is the Victorian campus of the **University of Glasgow**. The modern visitor may detect no major difference between the style of the main building and the grand buildings of the period elsewhere in the city, but in 1863–4 there was a fierce dispute when the commission to design it went to the English architect George Gilbert Scott, who, adding insult to injury, also gave the building contract to an English firm.

Also part of the university is the **Hunterian Museum**, based on the collections of curiosities, fossils and coins of a professor of medicine called William Hunter. This museum, with its famous coin collection, has won several prizes:

Map on pages 30–31

Below: a Buddha from the Burrell Collection
Bottom: the Burrell Collection interior

check whether there are any special exhibitions here while you are in Glasgow.

The ★ **Hunterian Art Gallery** consists of a collection of paintings and prints which was also started by Hunter but was continued after his death (and includes numerous works by Whistler and prints by Gauguin, Cézanne, Picasso, Kandinsky and Warhol). Mackintosh House is part of the complex and has reconstructed rooms from Mackintosh's own home.

CITY PARKS

For an old industrial city, Glasgow has a surprising number of open spaces, competing with London for the distinction of being the city with the largest park area relative to its size. On the far side of the once notorious areas known as the Gorbals and Govan (with the Glasgow Rangers football stadium, Ibrox Park, is the largest of the parks, the 363-acre (147-hectare) **Pollok Park**. The site of two important buildings with equally important art collections, Pollok Park is also very popular on fine days when Glaswegians picnic and enjoy the sun.

The two museums could not be more different from each other. The ★★ **Burrell Collection**, in its prize-winning modern building, is a conglomeration of precious objects from the collection of the shipbuilding magnate William Burrell. He invested his fortune in Chinese porcelain, antiques from the Mediterranean, Persian carpets and craftwork from medieval Europe. When he left it all to the city in 1944, he was concerned about the effects of industrial pollution on his treasures and stipulated that they be accommodated at least 15 miles (25km) outside the city. It was only in 1967 that his heirs agreed to have the collection housed in Pollok Park. This had just been made over to the city by Mrs Anne Maxwell Macdonald, together with ★★**Pollok House**, the neoclassical mansion belonging to her family, complete with its collection of Spanish paintings, including works by El Greco, Murillo and Goya.

MODERN ARCHITECTURE

By the docks to the west of the city centre are two impressive examples of contemporary architecture. On the northern bank of the Clyde is the **Scottish Exhibition Centre**, venue for concerts and exhibitions, with its 'Armadillo' building designed by Norman Foster. Almost opposite, on the south bank, is Glasgow's latest visitor attraction, the stunning, titanium-clad **Glasgow Science Centre**. This comprises three separate buildings, the revolving 400-foot (120-metre) Glasgow Tower, with views as far as Ben Lomond, the Science Mall, full of educational and interactive exhibits, and an IMAX cinema.

EXCURSION

Loch Lomond is Scotland's largest lake and one of the country's most popular beauty spots. It runs from north to south, surrounded by stunning mountain scenery, and has a total length of 23 miles (37km). In the south near the main towns of Alexandria and Balloch there are so many water sports facilities that the lake has become polluted and overcrowded. Not only is it on the itinerary of the many tourists who visit Scotland, but it is also the destination of thousands of daytrippers from nearby Glasgow.

Star Attractions
● The Burrell Collection
● Pollok House

Football Museum
In the southeast of the city is Hampden Park, the home of Scottish football, and also the location of the **Scottish Football Museum** (open Mon–Sat, 10am–5pm, Sun, 11am–5pm, closed on match days) which details the history of the game in Scotland, its social impact and issues surrounding the game, and also has displays of football memorabilia.

Pollok House

Map below

3: Aberdeen

For centuries Aberdeen was a centre of world trade, but today it is rather off the beaten track. Away from the main Highland routes, tourists must make a deliberate decision to visit, and ignore the unprepossessing outlying districts of the city with its minor industries and suburban estates. When looking for accommodation, visitors soon discover that the city is more interested in North Sea oil than in tourists. Unlike elsewhere, the hotels of Aberdeen are full during the week and advertise special offers at weekends.

Attracting visitors
The city is now promoting itself as a family holiday resort, and has plenty to offer the visitor: a distinctive appearance of granite buildings and flower beds; a long and varied history; several excellent museums; and a glimpse of the Scottish oil industry which since 1975 has made a major contribution to the British economy.

HISTORY

Aberdeen's ideal location at the mouth of the River Dee, with its natural harbour, made it an obvious place for settlement, and prehistoric settlers, Romans and Picts are known to have established themselves here. In the year 1136, because of its significance as a port, Aberdeen was granted the right to collect shipping duties, and in 1179 it became a Royal Burgh. In 1336–37 Edward III of England burned it to the ground and it was subsequently rebuilt on a much larger scale.

Old Aberdeen by the University

By 1495 Aberdeen already had a university, the third oldest in Scotland, and in subsequent centuries the city flourished as a major fishing and trading port. It was also the largest cattle market north of the Firth of Forth – the farmers drove animals here from as far as the Highlands of Wester Ross. During the Jacobite Risings of 1715 and 1745 the city officially supported the rebels, but kept its options open for the sake of peace and trade.

In the 18th and 19th centuries, colonial trade and the textile industry made Aberdeen prosperous. The harbour had to be enlarged, and in 1869, the Dee was diverted – in those days an unprecedented undertaking. Exactly 100 years later, another restructuring of the harbour took place in order to provide berths for ferries and ships supplying the North Sea oil rigs. With the oil boom the city regained its key position in the economic life of Scotland.

THE HARBOUR

The **harbour** ❶ is the city's focal point and its main source of income. It is accessible to visitors although some caution is advised. Early risers can experience the hustle and bustle as the night's catch is auctioned (before 7.30am) in the modern fish market on Albert Basin (Market Street). The history of the harbour is clearly documented in the ★**Maritime Museum** ❷, in Provost Ross's house on Shiprow, north of the Upper Dock. The house is interesting in itself, built in 1593 as the home of a wealthy merchant.

Below: Aberdeen pub life
Bottom: an oil support vessel in the harbour

CITY CENTRE

The inner city north of the harbour is dominated by two gigantic shopping centres, the Bon Accord Centre and the St Nicholas Centre. The **Kirk of St Nicholas** ❸ dates in part from the 12th century. During the Reformation the church was divided and used by both Catholics and Protestants. In the 17th century the eastern crypt was used for the imprisonment of women accused of witchcraft, who were attached by chains to the iron rings that can still be seen in the wall.

Map on page 38

The ★ **Aberdeen Art Gallery and Museum** ❹, on the corner of Blackfriars Street and Schoolhill, has an impressive collection of European paintings, mainly from the 18th to the 20th centuries, as well as works by a number of contemporary Scottish artists; the collection of Scottish silver and glass is also well worth seeing. ★ **Provost Skene's House** ❺ in Flourmill Lane, built in 1545 and the oldest house in the city, seems something of an anachronism crowded out by the shopping centres and office blocks. After careful restoration it is now a museum, with rooms decorated in the style of its various occupants down the centuries.

Below: Old Aberdeen, King's College
Bottom: Marischal College

MARISCHAL COLLEGE

★★ **Marischal College** on Broad Street was founded in 1593 in competition with the Catholic King's College. Rebuilt at the end of the 19th century, it has the distinction of being the second largest granite building in the world, after the Escorial Palace in Madrid. The extraordinary fretwork of pinnacles and gilt flags on the neo-Gothic facade make the unyielding substance of white granite seem almost delicate. One of the sections of the **University of Aberdeen Anthropological Museum** ❻ that is inside has exhibits relating to the prehistoric inhabitants of Scotland, in particular from the area around Aberdeen.

Other museums in the city are the **Cruickshank Botanic Gardens** belonging to the university, opposite St Machar's Cathedral in Old Aberdeen; the ★★**Satrosphere**, Justice Mill Lane south of Union Street (closed Tues), with hands-on science and technology exhibits.

Star Attractions
● **Marischal College**
● **Satrosphere**

THE NORTH

George Street or King Street, the main road which runs north behind Marischal College, will bring you to Old Aberdeen. On the parallel road, High Street, is **King's College**, the older of the two university colleges. The chapel dates from 1500 and contains the tomb of the university's founder, Bishop Elphinstone, to whom there is also a memorial in front of the building.

★**St Machar's Cathedral** is the oldest granite building in Aberdeen, which is often called 'Granite City'. It is worth taking a leisurely stroll though the area around the church with its old town houses, cobbled streets and air of unruffled solidity. The area extends to the ★**Brig o' Balgownie** over the River Don, the oldest Gothic bridge in Scotland, which is inevitably associated with a variety of legends *(see box)*.

> **Bridge legends**
> The popular hero Robert Bruce is said to have personally ordered the construction of the Brig o' Balgownie, and the mystic seer Thomas the Rhymer to have prophesied that it would collapse if a father with an only son ever rode across it on the only foal of a mare. Lord Byron, who went to school in Aberdeen, owned that as an only child he was afraid to cross the bridge.

CASTLE EXCURSION

Of the many aristocratic houses in the Aberdeen area, ★**Crathes Castle**, easily accessible on the A93, is probably the most popular (house, open Apr–Oct: daily from 10.30am; garden, all year from 9am). Built in 1553–94, with picturesque battlements, it not only has three rooms in the typical Scottish style but also a collection of ghosts, including the Green Lady. She is said to appear with her child – an infant's skeleton was found underneath a fireplace in one of the rooms she occupied.

The delightful gardens cover 593 acres (240 hectares) and are divided up into separate sections. They are as popular with Aberdonians as with tourists, and visitors are well catered for with a café, information centre and souvenir shop.

Crathes Castle

Map
on pages
42–43

Below: Brig o' Doon
Bottom: the Borders hills
near Moffat

4: The South

The Borders – Dumfries and Galloway – Ayrshire

In past centuries the Scottish border sometimes ran well south of the little town of Berwick-upon-Tweed, over which many battles were fought and which is now part of England. The traveller will certainly notice no radical changes in the landscape when crossing the border on the North Sea coast. The gently rolling hills only give way to more dramatic landscape further to the west.

The following route describes an arc from the east coast through the Southern Uplands to the Irish Sea in the west, and returns in a northeasterly direction to Edinburgh. Many visitors to Scotland simply pass this region by, but don't follow their example; the south has a great deal to offer.

THE LAMMERMUIR HILLS

The Great North Road (the A1) from London to Edinburgh crosses the Scottish border north of Berwick-upon-Tweed. This is the moment to leave the main road – to the west are the **Lammermuir Hills** with quiet minor roads through narrow valleys between high moorland hills.

One of the attractions on the southern edge of the Lammermuir Hills is **Manderston House** near Duns (open May–Sept: Thur, Sun and Bank Holiday Mon 2–5pm). It is a very fine example of an Edwardian country house dating from the early 20th century, although its severe neoclassical proportions actually go back to the end of the 18th century. The hemp and herring millionaire Sir James Miller who acquired it in 1900 only made a few alterations and extensions – the opulent marble cladding (even in the stables), silver staircase, thought to be unique, and spacious servants' quarters are all evidence of a degree of luxury that must have seemed completely anachronistic only a few years later.

The extensive gardens contribute to the overall lavish impression – as so often in Scottish gardens, rhododendrons are the speciality.

KELSO

Kelso is a typical small border town with a large market square at its centre. It is famous for its ruined **abbey**, located next to the parish church. This was once the largest and richest of the medieval abbeys in the southeast (the others being Dryburgh, Jedburgh and Melrose), of which only ruins remain. They were all destroyed in the 16th century, either during the dissolution of the monasteries ordered by Henry VIII, or the subsequent religious wars and wars of succession. Today, Kelso abbey is the least complete of all of them.

FLOORS CASTLE

★ **Floors Castle,** almost 2 miles (3km) northwest of Kelso (open Easter–Oct: daily 10am–4.30pm) is the magnificent country seat of the Dukes of Roxburghe. The house, begun in 1721 by William Adam and considerably enlarged in the 19th century by William Playfair, is the largest inhabited castle in Scotland, and became well-known all over the world when it featured as Tarzan's ancestral home in the 1984 movie *Greystoke*. There is a splendid view over the Tweed; the hill on the far side of the river was the site of one of the largest medieval fortresses in Scotland – although the little that remains of Roxburgh Castle is now barely visible from this distance.

Riverside retreat
To escape the crowds at Floors Castle, turn left off the road to the castle and head for the river. The grass-covered banks where the local people traditionally go to picnic and swim in the Tweed are known as The Cobby. Visitors should venture into the river for a refreshing dip only if they are strong swimmers.

Floors Castle opulence

Map
on pages
42–43

Literary figures

The borders' ruins of numerous castles and abbeys are a reminder of the constant disputes between the English and the Scots, but in around 1800 they had a romantic attraction for two of Scotland's most famous poets, both of whom settled in this area. Robert Burns spent the first years of his life in and around Ayr and his last years in Dumfries, while Walter Scott settled in Abbotsford House near Melrose. Many of Scott's novels are set in the borders.

THE ROXBURGHES

In this area it is impossible not to come into contact with the Roxburghe family: they own the best hotel for miles around, also called the Roxburghe, on the A698 at Heiton, 3 miles (5km) south of Kelso. The Victorian country house has an expensive appearance – but anyone who is not on a very restricted budget should make inquiries and might be pleasantly surprised. The food here is first-class and there are reasonably priced bar lunches.

★★**Melrose** is famous mainly for its ruined **abbey** (open June–Sept: daily from 10am; Mar–May and Oct: Mon–Sat from 10am, Sun from 2pm). The Cistercian monastery, founded in 1136, is in a more romantic setting than Kelso Abbey, and has the added attraction of the adjoining **Priorwood Gardens** (open Apr–Dec: Mon–Sat from 10am, Sun from 1.30pm).

On the other side is a garden where flowers and plants are grown for drying and pressing; the shop also sells delicious homemade jelly produced from the traditional varieties of apple grown in the adjacent orchard.

ABBOTSFORD HOUSE

Abbotsford House, 2 miles (3km) west of Melrose (open Mar–Oct: Mon–Sat from 10am, Sun from 2pm) is the country seat that Walter Scott

Melrose Abbey

had always wanted; he designed it himself and spent the last 20 years of his life here. The house makes a romantic impression, from the pseudo-medieval magnificence of the entrance hall to the inviting library with its many valuable tomes from Scott's own collection. It is easy to imagine him writing *Waverley, Ivanhoe* and *Kenilworth* here and in the neighbouring study. Some of these works were produced in a great hurry – his generosity as a host and his attempts to establish himself as a member of the landed gentry meant that he was constantly short of money and needed to keep producing books.

Star Attraction
● **Melrose**

SELKIRK

For an overnight stop it is worth making a detour to **Selkirk**. The place itself is a typical Borders town, best known for the fact that Walter Scott was sheriff here for more than 30 years. The court (today the Town Hall) dominates the market square and has a collection of Scott memorabilia.

Bowhill (3 miles/5km west of Selkirk on the A708) is a delight (house, open July only: daily 1–4.30pm; garden, late Apr–Aug: daily from noon, except Fri). The 18th-century estate is one of the many properties of the Dukes of Buccleuch, who are the biggest landowners in Scotland, and like all the family's houses, it is overflowing with treasures. In addition to the famous collection of portrait miniatures, there are important paintings by Raeburn, Gainsborough, Reynolds, Canaletto, Guardi, Claude Lorrain, Leonardo da Vinci and Ruysdael. There are also Louis-Quinze chairs with Aubusson covers, Meissen porcelain, hand-painted 18th-century Chinese wallpaper and much more besides.

Younger members of the family are catered for with an adventure playground containing wonderful tree houses, a riding stable, bicycles for hire and special paths for their use, footpaths to the nearby loch and the romantic ruin of Newark Castle, and the Bowhill Little Theatre next to the house, with a tiny stage and a varied programme. There is also a souvenir shop and a tearoom.

Selkirk market square

Map
on pages
42–43

Sweet tooth

Moffat, a friendly place on the road south to the Dumfries coast, is best known for the Toffee Shop on its spacious market square, where the world-famous Moffat Toffee is made and sold. This creamy confectionery is sold as sweets, but the real addicts buy it in bars.

An ideal overnight stop for families with children is **The Ley**, a very pleasant guesthouse (turn off the A72 at Innerleithen). Not far from here is **Traquair House**, which grew over the centuries from a simple 13th-century tower into an 18th-century castle (open July–Aug: daily 10.30am–5.30pm; Apr, May, Sept 12.30–5.30pm).

SPA TOWNS

★ **Peebles on the Tweed** is, deservedly, a tourist centre. It is well worth pausing en route to shop or visit a café (The Sunflower or Gino's Café de Luxe near the bridge), stay overnight in the vast Peebles Hydro hotel, or go for a walk in the Kailzie Garden or the Dawyck Botanic Garden, along the Tweed by the magnificently sited Neidpath Castle, or wander into Cardrona Forest.

Peebles Hydro and similar establishments are reminders that until well into the 19th century there were many spa towns in this area. In **Moffat**, for example, there is a well preserved bathhouse. From Moffat it is worth making a detour to the ★ **Grey Mare's Tail**, a spectacular waterfall 10 miles (16km) to the northeast with a fine, though strenuous, walk around it. The A708 from Selkirk to Moffat, past the waterfall and St Mary's Loch (with a stop at Tibbie Shiels Inn), is one of the most beautiful roads in the area.

DUMFRIES

Dumfries is the largest town in the southwest, with a population of 32,000; it is also the administrative centre of the Dumfries and Galloway region. It was formerly a place of strategic importance: several times in its history it was invaded and destroyed. Today, it is one of the focal points of the tourist industry that has been generated around the Scottish national poet, Robert Burns. Burns spent the last six years of his life in Dumfries, and his memory is kept alive by various memorials: ★ **Burns House**, where he died in 1796; the mausoleum over his grave in the cemetery of St Michael; the statue in the High Street;

Peebles on the Tweed

the memorabilia in his favourite pubs, the Globe Tavern and the Hole in the Wall; and in particular by the **Robert Burns Centre** in Mill Road (open Apr–Sept: Mon–Sat from 10am, Sun from 2pm; Oct–Mar: Tues–Sat from 10am). In the former mill there are audio-visual displays, models and other exhibits illustrating his life and work, as well as information about other places on the 'Burns Trail'.

Below: Burns statue
Bottom: an early printing

THE SOLWAY FIRTH

South of Dumfries is the beautiful coast on the **Solway Firth**, which is reasonably quiet, though swimming is not advisable owing to the high levels of radiation in the sea from the Sellafield reprocessing plant 31 miles (50 km) to the south.

A good road (A701/A711) takes you along the coast to Kirkcudbright, with some interesting features en route. While the ruins of **Sweetheart Abbey** in the village of New Abbey are not as imposing as those of Melros, they are well preserved, attractively sited and as crowded. The name goes back to the founder of the monastery, the pious (and rich) Devorguilla de Balliol, who was buried here in 1290 together with the embalmed heart of her beloved husband John. After his death at a young age she carried his heart around with her in a silver box.

Map
on pages
42–43

KIRKCUDBRIGHT

A little further off the main road is **Orchardton Tower** (signposted on the A711 south of Palnackie), the only round tower house in Scotland. It is thought to have been built in the 15th century by Irish builders, as Ireland has many such towers. The ruin is at first rather inconspicuous, as is its setting, but those who make the effort to climb the narrow winding staircase will not regret it.

This route takes us finally to **Kirkcudbright**, pronounced 'Kirkubree', on the estuary of the River Dee. As you drive through the green park-like landscape into this spacious town on a sunny day, you may well wish that you could stay here for longer. ★ **Broughton House**, the former home of the painter E.A. Hornel, is worth the stop alone.

There are many prehistoric sites dotted along the Solway Coast, the most impressive of which is to be found west of Gatehouse of Fleet: follow the signs on the A75 and walk uphill through the woods to the graves of ★ **Cairnholy I and II**.

Most people's first thought is that those who piled these stones one on top of the other 4,000 years ago must have been greatly in awe of death. A semicircle of upright stone slabs guards the narrow burial chamber of Cairnholy I, the entrance to which faces out over the open sea. During the excavations objects were found which must have been brought here from far away in Central and

Below: Kirkudbright vernacular architecture
Bottom: rural Galloway

Southern Europe, including bell beakers and parts of an axe made of jadeite. The slab of rock on top of the burial chamber of Cairnholy II would have needed many people to carry it here.

NEWTON STEWART

Newton Stewart is a good centre for a holiday in this region, with a good, quiet and reasonably priced hotel in the town itself (the Creebridge House Hotel). The peninsula to the south (The Machars) has two picturesque towns, **Wigtown** and **Whithorn**, beautiful beaches, peaceful countryside and numerous prehistoric and ancient sites. In addition to the Wren's Egg and Torhouse stone circles the excavations in Whithorn are particularly interesting. Whithorn Trust Discovery Centre in George Street (open Easter–Oct: Mon–Sat from 10.30am) runs guided tours and has an exhibition detailing the early Christian, Viking and medieval settlements.

GALLOWAY FOREST PARK

North of Newton Stewart is the **Galloway Forest Park**, a nature reserve 249sq miles (645sq km) in area, with good footpaths, a natural history information centre (Galloway Deer Museum at Clatteringshaws Loch), wild goat and deer enclosures and many other points of interest. There is even a special route for people who want to explore the forest without getting out of their car (Raiders Road, branching off the A712). West of Newton Stewart is ★ **The Rhinns of Galloway**. This peninsula, shaped like a hammerhead, is an area of great beauty with wide sandy beaches to the east and steep cliffs to the west, from which, on a clear day, Ireland seems very close.

From the coast road from Stranraer, north towards Ayr (A77/A719), there are magnificent views of the sea and the 1,115-ft (340-m) granite cone of **Ailsa Craig**. Once the place to which insubordinate monks were sent, the island is now reserved for its rightful inhabitants, and has become a bird sanctuary (boat trips from Girvan).

> **Smugglers' coast**
> In the village of Auchencairn, turn down the single-track road to Balcary Bay Hotel. The whole coast was once a notorious smugglers' paradise, especially since the Isle of Man was outside the sphere of the British customs authorities until 1876. In the 18th century, a commercial company established on the Isle of Man went so far as to build a supply cellar with a solid country house over it on this sheltered spot on the coast. Today this house is run as the Balcary Bay Hotel and at dusk, when staying in one of the fine rooms overlooking the bay, it is easy to imagine the smugglers' ships unloading their booty on the beach.

Galloway Forest deer

Map on pages 42–43

CULZEAN CASTLE

In Scotland, so many castles are a must on the tourist's list that it is difficult to find the right superlatives to do justice to ★★ **Culzean Castle** (open Apr–Oct: daily from 11am). It is neither particularly large nor particularly old, particularly historic nor particularly spectacular. But to drive past it would be to miss something absolutely unique. At Culzean (pronounced 'Collane'), between 1777 and 1792, Scotland's famous architect Robert Adam transformed a 16th-century tower house for the Kennedy family, producing an astonishing synthesis of neoclassical mansion and romantic castle. Although the exterior alone is well worth seeing, it is in the central staircase and the interior design of the rooms that Adam's genius is fully revealed, particularly the wonderful circular drawing room, with its ceiling in three pastel shades, a perfect example of Scottish Enlightenment elegance. The 18th-century-style park is also worth a visit (all year from 9.30am).

Below: Culzean Castle
Bottom: Ayr Auld Brig

The resorts on the coast between the Rhinns Peninsula and the Firth of Clyde range from old-fashioned, rather conservative **Troon** with its famous golf courses, to **Saltcoats** with its bingo halls, slot-machines and fairgrounds. They became suburbs of Glasgow in the summer in the days before cheap holidays abroad took their trade away.

AYR

The largest of all these resorts is **Ayr**. The broad sandy beaches are well-kept and apparently accommodate with ease the thousands of visitors who come here in the main season. Golf is the second major attraction of the town, and there are three fine courses. Ayr also has the most famous racecourse in Scotland and is a focal point for Robert Burns' devotees: his birthplace, Alloway, is now a suburb in the southern part of the town. The well-marked **Burns Heritage Trail** leads to the house where he was born (now a museum) and other places associated with the poet's life. Maps and guides can be obtained from the Tourist Information Centre *(see page 119)*.

The Fouters Restaurant in Academy Street, opposite the information centre, is hard to beat. The restaurant itself is very sophisticated, but the adjoining bistro is less formal, with little difference in the food. The Brig o' Doon Hotel in Alloway, close to the Burns House, is a pleasant place to stay, while for golfers Northpark House is located next to Belleisle, a frequently recommended course which is open to non-members.

NEW LANARK

From Ayr almost all roads lead to Glasgow (A77) or Edinburgh (A71), but there is a detour worth making: from the A72 turn off in the direction of Lanark to New Lanark and the **Falls of Clyde**. This is a popular destination for walkers. The scenery is very romantic, with the river tumbling over granite rocks, and the oaks and birches leaning over it veiled in the spray from the falls.

At ★ **New Lanark** on the banks of the Clyde, below the waterfall, is an open-air museum (visitors' centre, open all year from 11am). Here, in 1800, the industrialist David Dale and his son-in-law, reformer Robert Owen, embarked on what was then a revolutionary experiment: they set out to provide the workers in the cotton mills with proper housing, decent working conditions and educational facilities.

Star Attraction
● Culzean Castle

Marx on Owen
Karl Marx wrote of Owen's radical experiment, 'When Robert Owen... went beyond theoretical support for a restriction of the working day to 10 hours and put it into practice in his factory in New Lanark, this was derided as communist utopian thinking, as was also the link he established between productive work and child education, and the workers' cooperative stores that he founded'.

New Lanark village

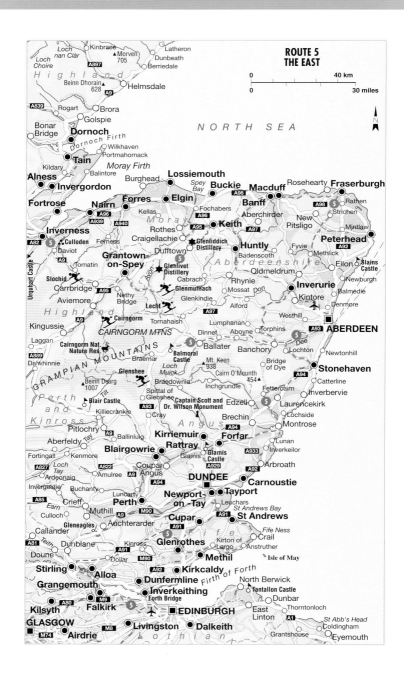

5: The East

Fife – Tayside – Grampian

There is no route through the eastern part of Scotland north of Edinburgh that does not reinforce the standard image of Scotland: golf, castles and whisky simply cannot be avoided. It is also in the east that the most famous names associated with each are to be found: the Old Course of St Andrews, Stirling Castle, Falkland Palace and the numerous distilleries of Speyside, the heartland of Scottish whisky production.

With the idyllic stretches of coast and the grandiose mountain landscape of the Cairngorms also on offer, the area provides a selection of Scotland's best tourist attractions.

From Edinburgh, the route described below leads, with a detour to Stirling, along the coast of Fife, with its pretty fishing villages, and then turns inland into the old county of Angus. South of Aberdeen it returns briefly to the North Sea, then bends round to the north, leading through the valleys of Speyside and finally on up to Inverness.

This is a classic holiday area (for the royal family as well as many of their subjects) and you are unlikely to find solitude. But the people who come here know what pleasures await them.

THE FIRTH OF FORTH

It is hard to leave Edinburgh without getting caught up in the jumble of motorways, dormitory towns and industrial estates on the south bank of the Firth of Forth. But this uninviting-looking area is not without its attractions: the impressive ★★ **Forth Rail Bridge**, for example, built in 1883–90, is one of the greatest engineering achievements of its time and still a conspicuous monument to progressive Victorian thinking.

A short distance to the west of the Forth Bridge is ★★ **Hopetoun House** (open Apr–Sept and Oct weekends: 10am–5.30pm), an interesting 18th-century manor house set in a large park on the banks of the Forth.

Map opposite

Star Attractions
● The Forth Rail Bridge
● Hopetoun House

A thankless task
Maintaining the Forth Bridge has become the ultimate in never-ending tasks — when the painters with their red anti-rust paint reach the end of the bridge it is said that they have to start again immediately at the other end.

The Forth Rail Bridge

Map on page 54

Battle of Bannockburn
The **Bannockburn Heritage Centre** can be found in the suburbs of Stirling near the M9/M80 intersection. A rotunda with an equestrian statue next to it commemorates the battle, in 1314, when Robert Bruce marshalled the Scottish troops to lead them to their bloodiest victory over the English: 'two counts, more than 60 barons and standard bearers, 268 knights and no less than 10,000 foot soldiers' on the English side lost their lives and King Edward II was forced to flee. The Battle of Bannockburn represented such a humiliating defeat for the arch enemy that it has become a symbol of Scottish independence.

Stirling Castle ramparts

STIRLING

The town of **Stirling** is dominated by its ★★ **Castle** (open Apr–Sept: Mon–Sat 9.30am–6.30pm, Sun from 2pm; Oct–Mar: Mon–Sat 9.30am–4.30pm, Sun from 2pm). Its impressive bulk is reminiscent of Edinburgh, as is its history: this royal residence saw the deaths of Alexander I (1124) and William the Lion (1214), the birth of James III in 1451 and the coronation of Mary Stuart as Queen of Scotland in 1543 at the age of nine months.

Most of the present building dates from the 15th and 16th centuries – further information about its colourful history is available in the Visitors' Centre on the Esplanade.

At the foot of the castle is the oldest and most attractive part of Stirling. In buildings such as **Argyll's Lodging** and the Guildhall, visitors are greeted in high season by people in period costume who give 'first-hand' accounts of the building's past history and occupants. The Ghost Walk is even more interesting: every evening in the summer 'the world of restless spirits and lost souls' comes to life around the castle (for details call TIC, tel: 01786 475019, or Heritage Events Co, tel: 01786 447150).

FIFE

From Stirling, head east to the **Fife Peninsula**. On the southern side of the Ochil Hills is **Dollar**, with the romantic **Castle Campbell** (open all year: Mon–Sat from 9.30am, Sun from 2pm) perched high above the woods of Dollar Glen. It is worth making the steep climb for the view over the Forth Valley. The walks along the stream, through the deciduous woods of the glen, are particularly beautiful in autumn, and for dedicated walkers there are longer trails through the Ochil Hills.

South of Auchtermuchty is Falkland with **Falkland Palace,** the hunting lodge of the Stuart dynasty (open Apr–Oct: Mon–Sat from 11am, Sun from 1.30pm). The guided tour of the palace, which was built between 1501 and 1542, not only takes in the reception rooms and private apartments, but also includes an explanation of Royal Tennis.

On the south coast of Fife is a string of attractive fishing villages, the largest of which is Anstruther, officially called the United Burgh of Kilrenny, Cellardyke, Anstruther Easter and Anstruther Wester, and referred to by the local people simply as Ainster. The **Scottish Fisheries Museum** on the harbour (open Apr–Oct: Mon–Sat from 10am, Sun from 11am; Nov–Mar: Mon–Sat from 10am, Sun from 2pm) gives a good picture of the history and practice of fishing on this coast, and also has two real fishing boats, moored next to the museum building.

In summer there are boat trips from Anstruther to see the puffins on the **Isle of May**. The 3½-mile (6-km) coastal path from Anstruther to the pretty harbour of Crail is also to be recommended.

ST ANDREWS

St Andrews is probably best known as the 'home of golf'. The Royal and Ancient Golf Club, founded in 1754, lays down the rules and history of the sport, and enthusiasts should visit the **British Golf Museum** opposite the clubhouse (open May–Oct: daily from 10am; Nov–Apr: closed Mon). St Andrews also has the oldest university in Scotland. From the 10th century, St Andrews was the seat of the most powerful bishop in Scotland, and had the largest cathedral in the country: the ruins of ★★ **St Andrews Cathedral**

Star Attractions
● **Stirling Castle**
● **St Andrews Cathedral**

Below: Anstruther harbour
Bottom: St Andrews Cathedral

Map
on page
54

Below: Scottish style
Bottom: Dunkeld Cathedral

at the end of South Street, still convey something of its former medieval splendour.

DUNDEE

Heading north, leave the Peninsula of Fife via the Tay Bridge, which will take you to **Dundee**, Scotland's fourth largest city. The two museum ships are worth a visit: the *RRS Discovery*, at the Discovery Centre, was the expedition ship of the South Pole explorer Robert Falcon Scott in 1901–04; the *HMS Unicorn* is a frigate with 46 cannons which was launched in 1824 – and illustrates the appalling conditions that were endured by sailors of the time. Otherwise, Dundee might be described, a little unkindly, as an endless suburb with a shopping centre in the middle.

PERTH

Perth is one of the most important towns in Scotland, and one of the nicest. A pleasant location on the River Tay close to the Highlands, a beautiful old centre, a good selection of cultural events and excellent shops all combine to make it a highly attractive place. It's no surprise, therefore, to learn that in 1990 it was selected as the town with the best quality of life in Great Britain.

PERTHSHIRE EXCURSION

From Perth a tour can be made, starting north along the A9, to **Dunkeld** and its fine ★ **Cathedral** beside the River Tay. Much of the building dates from the 15th century. Many of the old houses in Cathedral Street have been beautifully restored, making a lovely approach to the soaring ruins. Just north of Dunkeld is The Hermitage, with woodland walks leading to a folly overlooking the thundering Falls of Braan.

The A9 continues to **Pitlochry**, a busy tourist town. Its Festival Theatre stages plays from June to October. The power station at the artificial Loch Faskally features a salmon ladder, and is open to visitors (open Mar–Oct: daily from 10am).

A delightful path leads north (or take the B8079) to the ★ **Killiecrankie Visitor Centre**, which tells the story of the Jacobite victory here in July 1689. It also has much of interest on the natural history of the area. A short walk leads to the Soldier's Leap across a ravine (walks all year, visitor centre open Apr–Oct: daily from 10am).

Continue north to the charming village of **Blair Atholl** and ★ **Blair Castle**, the imposing home of the Dukes of Atholl, and also of the only private army in Britain, maintained by the Duke. The castle has fine furniture and paintings, and 32 of its rooms are open to view (open Apr–Oct: daily from 10am).

A short distance further north, the House of Bruar is a good craft centre and restaurant, with a walk to the spectacular **Falls of Bruar**. From here continue west on B847 to Kinloch Rannoch, at the east end of lovely Loch Rannoch, and then return on B846, skirting the superb mountain Schiehallion (the Fairy Hill of the Caledonians) to reach the town of Aberfeldy, past Castle Menzies, and across the wonderful old bridge built by General Wade in 1733. Next to it is a monument marking the founding of the Black Watch Regiment in the town.

From Aberfeldy, head south on the scenic A826 and A822 through the Sma' Glen, then turn east on A85 from Crieff to return to Perth.

Literary walk
There is a superb walk from Aberfeldy, up through the Birks of Aberfeldy, made famous by a poem by Robert Burns. The path leads to a fine waterfall. Birks are birch trees, but there is also an intriguing arboretum with many exotic tree species.

Blair Castle

GLAMIS

North of Dundee in the rolling hills of Angus (the home of the famous breed of cattle) is **Glamis** (pronounced 'Glahms'). The **Angus Folk Museum** (open Apr–Sept: daily 11am–5pm; Oct weekends only 11am–5pm) is a 19th-century row of terraced cottages. The carefully decorated interiors give an idea of the everyday life of the working population in this period.

The contrast between their living conditions and those of the aristocracy will be brought home to you all the more vividly if, after looking around the museum, you pay a visit to ★ **Glamis Castle**, a stately home surrounded by luxuriant gardens (open Easter–mid-Oct: daily from 10.30am). The seat of the Bowes-Lyon family, where the mother of the present Queen spent her childhood and Princess Margaret was born, Glamis is opulence itself. The building, dating to 1370, was transformed into a splendid manor house in the 17th century. There are said to be more ghosts within its walls than in any other building in Scotland.

> **Spectacular migrations**
> Montrose's unusual setting on the promontory that separates the Montrose Basin from the sea makes it a place of pilgrimage for birdwatchers, especially in winter, with huge flocks of wild geese arriving here from the Arctic from November onwards. It is worth going there in winter, on a clear, frosty day, just for the experience of walking from the Bridge of Dun, on the dyke, along the river to the point where it flows into the lagoon, with the noise of hundreds of birds coming in to land getting louder by the minute.

MONTROSE

Montrose is an attractive, friendly place on the North Sea coast with a busy harbour. Inland from Montrose are two interesting manor houses.

The **House of Dun** (3½ miles/6km west of Montrose) is surrounded by wooded land with marked trails. The house itself is a rather modest but perfect example of the neoclassical architecture created by the Adam family (open Easter, May, June and Sept: daily 1.30–5.30pm; July and Aug: daily 11am–5.30pm; Oct weekends: 1.30–5.30pm). As with all Adam buildings the interior is extremely stylish.

Fasque House north of Fettercairn (opening uncertain at present, tel: 01561 340 202 for current details) was designed to satisfy all the leisure requirements of upper-class Victorians. In addition to the deer park, the kitchen wing and the servants' quarters are particularly worth seeing. The memorabilia in the elegant rooms of the master and mistress are a must for anyone with an interest

Glamis Castle sitting room

in 19th-century history. From 1829 the house was owned by the Gladstone family, whose most famous member lived here when not in his official London residence – William Ewart Gladstone was British Prime Minister no fewer than four times between 1868 and 1894. In the 19th century he was the most important liberal statesman in Europe and Bismarck's most significant opponent.

Nothing could be a greater contrast to Fasque House than ★★ **Dunnottar Castle**, on the coast near Stonehaven (open Easter–Oct: Mon–Sat from 9am, Sun from 2pm; Nov–Mar: Mon–Fri from 9am). The extensive ruins, with the oldest building dating from the 14th century, are historically important, but it is the unique setting of this castle on top of a sheer cliff which first strikes the visitor. It is deservedly one of the most frequently photographed views in Scotland.

Stonehaven itself has a fine harbour. The Tollbooth Restaurant in its oldest building has excellent fish dishes and vegetarian food.

ROYAL DEESIDE

Inland is the region known as **Royal Deeside**, with the royal residence **Balmoral**. For monarchists and others curious about this peculiar aspect of British life, the castle, which was completed in 1855, is accessible from the A93 (ballroom and

Star Attraction
● **Dunnottar Castle**

Below: Balmoral
Bottom: Dunnottar Castle

gardens, open May–July: Mon–Sat from 10am). The royal family regularly spend the latter part of the summer here (during which time the castle is closed to the public) and unfailingly visit the ★★ **Highland Gathering** in Braemar on the first Saturday in September.

The best adjectives to describe the atmosphere of Banchory are 'solid' and 'respectable', and solid middle-class shops line the main road.

Below: traditional dance at the Highland Gathering
Bottom: the stone circle of Loanhead

INVERURIE

Continue in a northerly direction to **Inverurie**. The small museum in the Town Hall (open daily except Sun from 10.30am; closed 1.30–2.30pm and Wed afternoon) contains archaeological finds: the surrounding area has numerous prehistoric and ancient sites. On the hill known as **Bennachie** (1,739ft/530m), paths lead up through the woods and moors to the summit, with its fine view (accessible on the B9002 northwest of Inverurie).

On the nearby summit of **Mither Tap** is a well-preserved Iron-Age fort. There are signposts to sites associated with the Picts and other early settlers on all the roads leading north and west from Inverurie: Brandbutt Stone on the A96, Picardy Stone on the B9002 with Pictish symbols, and the **stone circle of Loanhead** on the B9001.

FRASERBURGH

Cross the attractive green countryside of the old county of Buchan (take secondary roads to appreciate it best) to rejoin the coast at **Fraserburgh**. While the place itself may not seem very inviting, the same can certainly not be said of the 3-mile (5-km) sandy beach in the bay, which is exceptionally clean. The lighthouse of Kinnaird Head was built in 1787 from the tower of the castle which stood on this spot – it is said to be the oldest lighthouse in Scotland. It now houses a fascinating museum. From here follow the north coast via Rosehearty, with its attractive campsite by the sea, and the imposing ruins of Pitsligo Castle, past the cliffs of Pennan Head and

Troup Head and through the rather inconspicuous fishing harbour of Macduff to Banff.

In spite of its many visitors, **Banff** has maintained an aura of unruffled sophistication, to
which several buildings by the Adam family have
contributed: the simple Town House (town hall,
built in 1767) is by John or James Adam, and
Banff Palace is by William Adam, as is the elegant **Duff House** in a park south of the centre.

THE WHISKY TRAIL

Away from the coast are the numerous distilleries
on the ★ **Malt Whisky Trail** southwest of Banff.
The pagoda-like chimneys of the oast houses
around Keith and Dufftown will soon become
familiar landmarks, and many distilleries offer
tours and a taste of the product – Glenfiddich in
Dufftown (open Mon–Sat 9.30am–4.30pm; Apr–
Oct also Sun noon–4.30pm) and Glenlivet, near
the village of the same name (open Mar–Oct:
Mon–Sat 10am–4pm, Sun 12.30–4pm) cater particularly well for visitors. Excellent single malt
whisky is also produced by Cragganmore, in
Ballindalloch on the River Spey (tel: 01807
500202 for opening times).

South of Glenlivet in the heart of the Grampian
Mountains, take the time to stop for a while in
Tomintoul, one of the highest villages in the

Star Attraction
● The Highland Gathering

> **Different distillery**
> It is not whisky that is dis-
> tilled in Blanchory but
> lavender, in order to make perfume.
> The distiller is called Ingasetter: it
> offers tours on weekdays from 10am
> and also has a shop.

Glenfiddich distillery

Below: Boat of Garten sign
Bottom: Strathspey Railway

Highlands. Take a break from travelling, drink in the scenery and perhaps go for a walk along the river or up into the hills, then drive in a westerly direction to return to the Spey Valley.

Boat of Garten is tourist-oriented. Along the two major roads (A9/A95) in the valley there is a constant stream of hikers, climbers, mountain bikers and canoeists, anglers and golfers, and, with the first fall of snow, skiers heading for Aviemore and Cairngorm. At **Loch Garten** nature reserve a round-the-clock watch is kept to ensure the survival of the ospreys which breed here every year. The steam trains of the **Strathspey Railway** run through the beautiful countryside between Boat of Garten and Aviemore, and along the 'Ski Road' from Coylumbridge to the Cairngorm lifts is the **Glen More Forest Park**.

CULLODEN

Follow the main road to Inverness a short way and at the village of Daviot take the signposted turning to the ★ **Battlefield of Culloden**. We began this route at the scene of a decisive Scottish victory (Battle of Bannockburn), and end it at the scene of the crushing defeat which put an end to hopes of Scottish influence in Great Britain. The visitors' centre is open all year round (open Apr–Oct: from 9am; Nov–Mar: from 10am), but the best impression of the place is obtained early in the morning on the battlefield itself.

On 16 April 1746, the last battle on British soil was fought between some 5,000 exhausted Highlanders under the leadership of the Stuart Pretender to the throne, Bonnie Prince Charlie, and 9,000 members of the Duke of Cumberland's elite troops. The Highland Scots were at the end of their strength after their campaign, and Cumberland was a much more experienced commander.

Around 1,200 Highlanders are said to have fallen in the battle, and Cumberland acquired the nickname 'the butcher' when he gave orders to massacre all the wounded left on the field, plus the onlookers who had come to the scene from Inverness.

INVERNESS

Inverness, often called the 'Capital of the High-lands', has recently acquired city status. This, by far the largest centre of population in the far north, with more than 40,000 people, is the administrative centre of the huge but thinly-populated Highland Region. It also has the best selection of shops for miles around. The railway lines from Edinburgh and Aberdeen, the line to Kyle of Lochalsh in the east, and the only line to the north (Wick/Thurso) all converge at Inverness, and the town is correspondingly busy. Car drivers should note that parking in the centre is difficult and the one-way system can be confusing.

Nessie tours
It is now possible to take an expensive trip by submarine through the loch, which reaches a depth of 984ft (300m). Boat trips on the surface are offered from Inverness, Fort Augustus or Drumnadrochit.

LOCH NESS

Inverness means 'mouth of the Ness'. Follow the river in a southwesterly direction to reach ★★**Loch Ness**. Although the originator of the most famous photo of the monster recently confessed just before his death that it was a fake, this has not so far done any harm to the tourism generated by 'Nessie'. Two competing monster information centres can be found in Drumnadrochit.

On the busy A82, after leaving the loch, it is almost impossible to miss the dramatically-sited ruins of **Urquhart Castle** (open Mon–Sat from 9.30am, Sun from 2pm).

Below: a plastic Nessie
Bottom: Urquhart Castle

ROUTES 6 & 7
THE NORTHWEST
AND HEBRIDES

0   40 km
0   30 miles

N

Butt of Lewis
Lionel
Skigersta
Cellar Head
A857
North Tolsta
Arnol   Barvas
7
Carloway   Broad Bay
Coll   Portnaguran
Lewis
Gallan Head   Newmarket
Uig   Callanish
Crulabhig   Bayble
Achmore   STORNOWAY
Brenish   Loch   Banish
Langavat   ST. Columba's Church
Scarp   Balallan
7
Hushinish   Kebock Head
Clisharn   Ardvourlie Lemreway   Reiff
Scalpay   800   ▲Beinn Mhor   Summer
Taransay   671   Isles
Seilebost   Tarbert
Toe Head   Scalpay Shiant
Harris   Manish   Islands   The Minch   Cove   Laide
Pabbay Berneray   Leverburgh   Fionn
Boreray   Rodel   Melvaig   Loch
Tigharry Sollas Newtonferry   Kilmaluag   Poolewe Gairloch
Balranald   Lochmaddy   Kilmuir   Quiraing   Redpoint   Talladale
North   Trumpan   542 Staffin   Beinn
Trinity Temple   Uist   Loch   Uig   Eighe▲
Balivanich   Clo Mor Snizort Kilt Rock   Fearnmore   1009
7   Ronay   Lusta Old Man   Torridon   6
Creagorry Benbecula Boreraig Edinbane of Storr Rona   Shieldaig
Hornish Point   Wiay   Milovaig   Kensaleyre Beinn Bhan   Strathcarron
Our Lady of the Isles   Dunvegan   Portree Tornapress   ▲895   Stromeferry
Stilligarry   South   Bracadale   Skye   Raasay Toscaig
Uist   The Braes   Scalpay   Plockton 6
Flora   ▲Beinn Mhor Portnalong   A850   Kyle of   Eilean
Macdonald's 620   Sligachan   Broadford Lochalsh   Donan
Birthplace   Dalibergh Bualintur Cuillins   Kyleakin Castle
Lochboisdale Torrin   Shiel
Ludag   Soay Elgol Isleornsay   Bridge
Sound of Barra   Cuillin   Tarskavaig Arnisdale
Eriskay   Canna Kilmory Sound Ardvasar Ladhar Kinloch
Barra   Cuillin Sound   Bheinn Hourn
Kisimul   7   1019
Castle Castlebay Rum   Mallaig Ben Aden
Vatersay   Harris▲   885
Sandray   Cleadale A830
Rosinish   Eigg   Sound of Lochailort
Mingulay   Sea of The Hebrides   Muck Eigg Arisaig Inverailort
Sound of   Castle
7   Arisaig Castle Tioram Loch
Portuairk   Acharacle   Shiel
Sorisdale   Mingary   Salen Strontian
Coll   Arinagour Castle   A861
Tobermory   Creach
Arileod   Loch   Bheinn
Tiree Caoles Dervaig Drimnin Sunart 853
Loch   Portnacroish
Frisa   Oban

Inner Sound
Sound of Raasay
Inner Sound
The Little Minch
The Minch
Sound of Harris
Sound of Monach
Outer Hebrides
Sea of The Hebrides
Inner Hebrides
Sound of Sleat

Map
on pages
66–67

6: The North

Ross and Cromarty – Sutherland – Caithness

The far north of Scotland has no equivalent. Soon after leaving Inverness, the distance between the villages and towns increases, and once you have reached the rugged Atlantic Coast in the west you will find empty beaches even in high season. Away from main roads you may travel for hours without seeing an inhabited house. Fjord-like lochs penetrate deep into the country from the sea, along with numerous freshwater lakes; every now and then, however, the pattern is broken by a massive rocky peak such as Suilven, which dominates the surrounding landscape.

Castles and palaces are rare in the west (with the exception of the odd picturesque ruin), and the region sometimes has the deceptive feel of somewhere waiting to be discovered.

Just how populated this now deserted area once was is indicated by the fact that in 1854, at Wester Gruinards, 70 women (whose husbands were either fighting in the Crimean War or had deserted), attempted to resist one of the last clearances in the county and were beaten up by land agents and constables – contemporary reports state that 20 women and girls were seriously injured.

The suggested route follows the coast, with a few detours into the interior, and takes you to

Colonial crimes
To get an idea of what the rural population suffered during the Highland Clearances, take the road that leads from Ardgay, west of Tain, through Strathcarron Valley to the little church of Croick. In the spring of 1845, a handful of families who had been forced off their rented land in Glencalvie took refuge here, and the messages that they scratched in the glass of the church windows, which are still easy to decipher, bear clear testimony to their suffering.

Rainbow across the Black Isle

the end of the mainland in the northeast and to Kyle of Lochalsh, the gateway to Skye, in the southwest. Motorised travellers are at an advantage in this region: trains only go to the east coast, buses primarily serve the main routes, and cyclists must be fit to tackle the roads here (although they will be greatly rewarded by parts of this route).

THE BLACK ISLE

The bridge over the **Moray Firth** north of Inverness leads onto the peninsula known as the **Black Isle**, an attractive area with woods in the centre and fine beaches, that is often neglected by travellers speeding past on the A9. The bird sanctuaries of Munlochy Bay and Udale Bay, with their many different species of wader, are well-known to birdwatchers, and the fishing village of ★ **Cromarty** on the northeastern tip of the peninsula, tidied up for the tourists in recent years, is extremely attractive. In order to include these sights on your tour, take the first turning north on the far side of the bridge – it is not necessary to drive right round the peninsula as there is a car ferry from Cromarty to Nigg on the Fearn Peninsula (half-hourly service between 9am and 6pm, for more information call Seaboard Marine, tel: 01862 871255). In Cromarty Firth you may see an oil rig in tow passing by – it is in this region that they are constructed and maintained.

DORNOCH

North of the pretty town of Tain, the A9 follows the shore of **Dornoch Firth**. **Dornoch**, on the north shore of the bay, is a small, pleasant place, its most important attribute being its main square, which has a restored church and the remains of a bishop's palace dating from the 16th century, which today forms part of the pleasant Dornoch Castle Hotel. The famous Royal Dornoch Golf Course lies on the dunes to the south. Golf has been played here since the early 17th century and the present course, designed in 1877 by Tom Morris senior, is well-known among keen golfers.

Below: Inverness Castle
Bottom: Dornoch church

Map
on pages
66–67

*Below: Dunrobin Castle
Bottom: the fishing fleet
at Helmsdale*

DUNROBIN

From Dornoch, follow the east coast to the north. If withdrawal symptoms set in when the daily itinerary does not include a castle, a quick visit to ★ **Dunrobin Castle** near Golspie is recommended (open Easter and May–Oct: Mon–Sat 10am–5.30pm, Sun from noon; June–Aug: Sun from 10.30am; gardens open all year round from 9.30am). The seat of the Dukes of Sutherland, who played a leading part in the Highland Clearances, it is full of magnificent art objects and furniture. The original building, dating from the 13th century, was enlarged and transformed into this showy château in 1845–50.

The most interesting of the resorts on this coast is ★ **Helmsdale**. The history of the Highlands is presented very clearly at the Timespan Centre (open Easter–Oct: Mon–Sat from 10am, Sun from 2pm) with tableaux, sound effects and audio-visual displays. Among the aspects covered are the lives of the Picts and Vikings, a legendary murder in Helmsdale Castle and the clearances in the area. One of the main topics is the gold rush, which started at the end of the 19th century when this precious metal was discovered in the Strath of Kildonan. The Tourist Information Centre advertises Goldrush Heritage Tours to the places where it was found. Helmsdale is also the last place that the northbound train follows the coast before turning inland; it then follows a magnificent scenic route and only returns to the coast at Wick or Thurso.

WICK

The part played by Scandinavian invaders and settlers in the history of the far north of Scotland can be seen from the place names alone; this is nowhere more obvious than in **Wick** – a name derived from the Nordic word *vik* (bay, estuary, trading centre), which is also the stem of Viking. Wick is a busy town with a population of around 8,000 and is equipped to cope with any number of tourists. The Heritage Museum gives a vivid picture of the history of fishing in the region. Looking at the quiet harbour today it is hard to believe old photos which show it filled with hundreds of fishing boats – more than 1,100 herring boats are said to have been based here in the past.

The lighthouse of **Noss Head** north of Wick is worth a visit. Nearby on the cliffs above Sinclair's Bay are the impressive ruins of **Sinclair and Girnigoe Castle**, which has a tragic tale attached to it. In the 16th century the fourth Earl of Sinclair is said to have suspected his son of wanting to murder him, and had the young man imprisoned here, where he apparently died in the dungeon seven years later 'lice-ridden and starved'. It is said that the sounds of his wailing and groaning can still be heard in the castle walls. Access to the ruins is rather unsafe and you are advised to take care.

JOHN O'GROATS

From the harbour of **John o' Groats** there are boat trips to **Orkney**, to the nearby island of **Stroma** and the cliffs of ★ **Duncansby Head**. The trips feature romantic rock formations, seals, huge colonies of birds – and a rough sea, which may spoil the day for some. Although John o' Groats is always known as the northernmost point of the British mainland, Dunnet Head, high above the sea, with a view across to Orkney on a clear day, is further north.

Cairns and menhirs
After the village of Lybster watch out for the turn-off to Camster and Watten. This road leads to the **Grey Cairns**, two well-preserved, impressive burial cairns from 2500BC. They are marked with explanatory signs and it is possible to peer inside. To the southeast, near the coast road, is the **Hill o' Many Stanes**, a complex dating from the early Bronze Age with approximately 200 menhirs arranged in the shape of a fan – it is still not known exactly what their function was.

Duncansby Head

Map on pages 66–67

Dounreay
One feature of the area should be mentioned: the atomic power plant Dounreay (Thurso owes its well-stocked shops to the custom generated by employees of this establishment). The 'fast breeder' was closed down in March 1994 but the reprocessing of spent fuel continued, even after the management admitted to depositing radioactive waste in a shaft which was threatened by erosion and might have collapsed into the sea. In 1998 the decision was made to close the plant, after all nuclear material remaining on the site has been processed.

Cape Wrath

Some of the most spectacular scenery in Europe is to be found along the north coast of Scotland. The main road keeps leaving the coast so you must take every minor road to the right if you are not to miss views of lonely bays, rugged cliffs, roaring breakers, seabirds gliding in the wind and distant islands in the mist. On the stretch between John o' Groats and Durness take, as a very minimum, the turnings to Strathy Point, Armadale, Torrisdale/Skerray and Talmine/Midfield.

THURSO

One of the most attractive places on this stretch of coast is **Thurso**, with good shopping facilities and Scrabster Harbour, where car ferries leave for Stromness on the main Orkney island.

Bettyhill is a pretty village in magnificent surroundings; on the other side of the little bay is the Invernaver Nature Reserve, with many different species of plants and birds. The Strathnaver Museum (open Apr–Oct: Mon–Sat from 10am) in a former church gives a good impression of the clearances in the valley south of the village: this detour of around 37 miles (60km) is well worth making if time permits. The road through the historic Strathnaver Valley brings you to a junction at the end of Loch Naver, where you will find the Altnaharra Hotel, to be recommended for its superb location and much else besides.

From here, take either the road north which joins the coast at the charming village of Tongue, or the adventurous-looking road northwest which skirts Ben Hope, Scotland's northernmost Munro *(see page 115)*. It is a long and difficult hike to the top of the 3,041-ft (927-m) summit, and one which should be undertaken only with the proper equipment, but the view is worth the effort.

CAPE WRATH

The road follows the shore of the idyllic **Loch Eriboll**, a large bay that stretches back a long way inland, and eventually arrives at **Durness**, which has several rather special features: the impressive

Smoo Cave, a limestone cave with a high, easily accessible outer chamber; the craft colony of Balnakeil and the famous cliffs of ★★ **Clo Mor** on Cape Wrath. The cape can only be reached by passenger ferry from Keoldale followed by a 30-minute drive in a minibus – exploring on your own is discouraged as the whole area is used by the British army as a shooting range – but the view is wonderful.

Star Attraction
● Clo Mor

SANDWOOD BAY

For dedicated hikers the most beautiful walk in Scotland is the one from **Cape Wrath** south to **Kinlochbervie**. It should not, however, be undertaken lightly: the 17-mile (28-km) trail is lonely and most of it far from any road, so there is no possibility of breaking off in the middle.

However, it does take you along the legendary beach of **Sandwood Bay**, which cannot be reached by car. From the far end of the path, which comes from the south behind Kinlochbervie, it is still nearly 4½ miles (7km) to Sandwood Bay (signposted from Balchrick – reckon on three hours there and back), which ensures that the bay is not overrun with visitors. This is just as well, since this is where mermaids from all around come ashore to rest, a fact reliably confirmed by the local shepherds.

Below: Smoo Cave
Bottom: Sandwood Bay

Map
on pages
66–67

Climbing Suilven

The best road to take on leaving Lochinver is the one that runs between the coast and the impressive peak known as **Suilven**. This road is described in so many guidebooks as one of the most beautiful on the west Highland coast that it is no longer a well-kept secret, and there is more traffic in the main season than the single-track road can really cope with. But this does not make the description any less accurate or the route less attractive. Suilven is climbed every year by numerous mountain hikers; it is not a difficult climb but it is a long one – experienced hikers should allow eight hours there and back from the nearest car park (Glencanisp).

THE WEST COAST

From here the route turns south down the west coast, and here the same principle applies as on the north coast: if you stick to the well-made main road and ignore the narrow side roads, you will not discover the real beauty spots of Scotland.

From Tarbet, north of the small resort of Scourie, there are boat trips to the **bird sanctuary** on **Handa Island**. The 15-minute ride (Apr–Sept: Mon–Sat) brings you into close contact with thousands of gulls, guillemots, razorbills, fulmars and cormorants. After the bridge at Kylestrome (until 1984 there was a romantic ferry ride at this point), the B869 turns off to the Point of Stoer and **Lochinver**. Stop for a meal at the Riverside Bistro as you enter the village on the main road – the food is good and they cater for vegetarians.

Once on the peninsula of **Coigach,** turn right to get to the beach on Enard Bay near Achnahaird (with an idyllically located campsite). In the south of the peninsula is ★ **Achiltibuie**, a long line of houses with a view of the **Summer Isles**. Next to the Summer Isles Hotel is the **Hydroponicum**, often described as the garden of the future (open Apr–Oct: guided tours at 10am, 12pm, 2pm and 5pm). Here exotic plants are grown in adjustable microclimates and hydrocultures, with solar cells providing the necessary energy.

Ullapool fishing boat

ULLAPOOL

From Achiltibuie return to the main road to continue towards the south. A turning off the A835 will take you to the **Inverpolly Nature Reserve**, near Knockan, which has an information centre and nature trail (centre open May–Sept: daily from 10am). Continue south to the main centre of the region, **Ullapool**. During the main season the town is often very full, but Ullapool does have a number of attractions, including the campsite on the tongue of land jutting out into **Loch Broom** in the middle of the town. Above this is the charming and slightly eccentric Ceilidh Place, a combination of restaurant and café, hotel and function centre, and on the other shore of Loch Broom is the world-famous Altnaharrie Inn, the only restaurant in the northwest of Scotland with a Michelin star and one of the few that can only be reached by private boat. This fact, combined with the prices and the necessity to stay overnight, ensures that no-one strays by chance into this exclusive enterprise.

Boat trips to the Summer Isles are strongly recommended (there are several organizers at the harbour), during which, in addition to the superb scenery, you will see cormorants, seals, (with a bit of luck) dolphins and occasionally (with even more luck) a whale. From Ullapool there is also a car ferry to **Stornoway** on the Hebridean Island of **Lewis** (in summer Mon–Sat three times a day; the crossing takes about 3 hours).

INVEREWE

The fjord-like bays in this area go so far inland that the drive along the coast involves constant detours, but this is more than compensated for by the splendid views along the way. It is easy to be so distracted by all this wonderful scenery that you miss recommended sights such as ★ **Inverewe Gardens** on Loch Ewe, north of Poolewe (garden, open all year from 9.30am; visitors' centre/souvenir shop closed in winter; guided tours

Below: Inverewe Gardens
Bottom: view across
the Summer Isles

Map on pages 66–67

Loch Maree

Loch Maree, southeast of Gairloch, is said to be the most beautiful lake in Scotland. Some might dispute this, but the scenery is certainly outstanding. At Talladale is the Loch Maree Hotel, which is particularly popular with anglers, and at the southern end of this long lake is the visitors' centre of the Beinn Eighe National Nature Reserve, which provides information about the flora and fauna of this extensive reserve, and is the starting point of two nature trails, both of which lead through the old Caledonian forest.

Loch Maree

mid-Apr–mid-Sept: Mon–Fri 1.30pm). On this piece of land, apparently, nothing was growing but a solitary willow tree when, in 1862, Osgood Mackenzie started to lay out a garden with exotic plants from all over the world. Today the gardens are justifiably the major tourist attraction on this coast, now occupying more than 20 acres (49 hectares) of land, and interlaced with paths which take several hours to explore.

GAIRLOCH

Gairloch has been catering for tourists since the 19th century. The award-winning **Heritage Museum** documents the life of the region's people since the Stone Age, and the Mountain Restaurant is a recommended place to eat, especially for vegetarians. Explore some of the minor roads to the beaches and vantage points: the B802 leads north to the appropriately named Big Sands, while the B8056 in the south will take you to Redpoint, with a splendid view of the **Isle of Skye**.

THE APPLECROSS PENINSULA

To explore the peninsula of **Applecross** start at Shieldaig, an idyllic place (with its highly commended pub and hotel, Tigh-an-Eilan). The only road takes you along the coast (with wonderful views of the islands of Rona and Raasay). Between the road and the shore there is the occasional ruined cottage – although it is hard to believe, according to parish records there were still almost 2,900 people living here in the first half of the 19th century. In Applecross itself, which consists of two houses, a shop with a café, a public toilet and a campsite, take the narrow road branching off inland, which climbs steeply and finally reaches the top of ★★ **Bealach na Bà** pass at over 600m (2,000ft). The Gaelic name means Cattle Pass, and it was along this magnificent route that cattle were once driven to market. Today motorists come to enjoy the splendid view across to the mountains of Skye before embarking on the perilously steep descent into the valley.

KYLE OF LOCHALSH

From the south side of the Bealach na Bà pass,
the attractive town of **Plockton** can be seen far
below on the far side of Loch Carron, but the road
winds for miles round the loch before it actually
gets there. Plockton's particular attraction is its
promenade along the shore, against the backdrop
of a hillside lined with houses painted in white
and pastel colours. The palm trees thrive in the
mild climate of the sheltered bay, in which numerous yachts lie at anchor. A good place to stay is
the Haven Hotel, which is as charming as the
village itself.

Star Attraction
● Bealach na Bà

  Kyle of Lochalsh is still the gateway to the Isle
of Skye for the majority of visitors. The approach
to the controversial, if impressive, new toll bridge
over the strait of Loch Alsh, which was opened
in 1995, bypasses the town, and visitors now
drive straight across to Kyleakin on the other side
(see page 80).

Below: Eilean Donan Castle
Bottom: Plockton

  To the east of Kyle of Lochalsh, on the main
road through to Fort William *(see page 90)*, is
★ **Eilean Donan Castle**, proudly standing on a
rocky peninsula at the confluence of Loch Duich,
Loch Alsh and Loch Long. For a long time there
was only a ruin here, and it was not until the
beginning of the 20th century that restoration was
commenced – today it is one of the most photographed subjects in Scotland.

Map
see
front

ORKNEY AND SHETLAND

The collection of islands that comprise Orkney have much to offer, the main attractions include some of the best archaeological remains in Europe, and wonderful natural history and landscapes.

Kirkwall, the islands' capital, has the 12th-century **St Magnus Cathedral**, and also the ★ **Bishop's Palace** and **Earl's Palace**, which together provide a snapshot of Orkney history (open all year, daily, Sun afternoon only). **Highland Park** is the most northerly distillery in Britain (visitor centre open Apr–Oct: daily from 10am), while at **Hatston**, the Ortak Visitor Centre (open all year daily) sells outstanding Orkney jewellery.

Below: nesting seabirds
Bottom: Orkney's wild coast

ORKNEY EXCURSIONS

The islands are connected by truly excellent ferry services which make getting around easy. However, on Mainland (the biggest island), you must visit ★★ **Skara Brae**, the oldest surviving village in Europe, a Stone Age settlement dating back 5,000 years. The visitor centre has lots of background information (open Apr–Oct: daily from 10am). **Maes Howe** is regarded as probably the finest chambered tomb in Western Europe, and a guide will show you the Viking 'graffiti' inside. The nearby **Ring of Brodgar**, a stone circle, have a powerful and unique atmosphere.

To the south is the island of **South Ronaldsay**, with the ★ **Italian Chapel** made by prisoners of war in the 1940s, while a ferry from Stromness, in west Mainland, goes over to **North Hoy**. A strenuous but magnificent walk leads across Hoy to the **Old Man of Hoy** rock pillar.

Rousay has an RSPB bird reserve with a good circular walk, and if you want to be really adventurous you can take the flight from Kirkwall, which includes in its itinerary the shortest commercial air journey in the world. Linking the islands of **Westray** and **Papa Westray**, it lasts under two minutes and is not for the faint-hearted, as the approach is over cliffs to a rough grass field.

SHETLAND

Shetland is as far north in Britain as you can get. This means in summer the daylight is almost endless, a twilight known as the 'simmer dim', lasting for about three hours around midnight before the sun rises again in the north-east. But the Shetland year begins in January with the annual **Up Hell**, a festival in which a replica Viking longboat is dragged through the streets of the capital, **Lerwick**, before being ceremonially burnt.

The long thin island called Mainland stretches from the cliffs at **Sumburgh Head**, up to the **Point of Fethaland**, a distance of over 60 miles. Near Sumburgh is ★ **Jarlshof**, an archaeological and historical site with an intriguing mix of remains dating over many centuries and with superb sea views (all year, daily from 10am). On the way to Lerwick is the small island of **Mousa** with the most complete *broch* (circular fortified tower) in Scotland. There are boat trips to it in summer from **Sandwick**.

Lerwick also has a *broch*, called **Clickhimin**, and **Fort Charlotte**, a 17th- to 18th-century barracks overlooking the harbour, with views to the island of **Bressay**, reached by ferry and noted for its birdlife and seals. A short distance west of Lerwick is **Scalloway**, with the ruined **Earl Patrick's Palace**, built in the 17th century (open Mon–Sat from 10am, Sun from 2pm).

Star Attraction
● Skara Brae

The furthest north
The opportunity to head as far north as possible is irresistible. Crossing the island of **Yell** leads to a second short ferry over to **Unst**. At the northern end of Unst is ★ **Hermaness Nature Reserve**. From the end of the road a walk of 4 miles (6.5km) leads to **Herma Ness** itself, looking across to the rocky islet of Muckle Flugga with its lighthouse. This is truly the end of Britain: north is the Arctic Ocean. The reserve is noted for its 'bonxies' – large gulls which are fiercely protective of their territory and are quite likely to make repeated passes at intruders.

Shetland fiddler

Map
on pages
66–67

7: The Hebrides

Skye and the Outer Hebrides

The Outer Hebrides are a holiday destination in themselves, not only for the sea trip, which makes all the islands except Skye seem distant from the mainland, but also because of their individual character. In addition, their landscape and language set them apart. Skye is so close to the west coast of Scotland that it is hardly an island – and the new road bridge makes it seem even more like part of the mainland.

Below: a hillside inhabitant
Bottom: view to Skye from
the Kyle of Lochalsh

ISLAND HOPPING

The first part of the following route will take you to the dramatic peaks of the Cuillins of Skye and sites connected with the island's varied history. From Uig in the northwest the ferry leaves for Tarbert on Harris. In less than two hours you are in a different world; all the street names are in Gaelic, island life comes to a standstill on Sunday, and the weather is unpredictable even by Scottish standards.

The journey then continues by ferry from Harris to North Uist and along the embankments to Benbecula and South Uist. A further short crossing brings you to Barra and from here there is a ferry service to Oban back on the mainland.

Not all the inhabited islands of the Hebrides can be included here, but the suggested route will give you an idea of the largest and most developed of them. Having visited once, it is likely that you will be back again for more.

Star Attraction
● **Skye**

SKYE

As soon as the new bridge (scene of many protests by locals over the high tolls) from Kyle of Lochalsh to Kyleakin on ★★ **Skye** was completed, the trusty car ferry that had plied its way back and forth for so long went out of service. Kyleakin is where most holidaymakers arrive on the island, but there are other ways of getting there: from Mallaig, south of Skye, there is a car ferry to Armadale seven times a day (crossing time is approximately 30 minutes); this is also the terminus of the railway line from Glasgow/Fort William.

There is also a short, summer-only ferry crossing from Glenelg to Kylerhea, and although this can only be reached by single-track road from Shiel Bridge, the drive is one of the most beautiful in the area. The Glenelg Inn is a must and the Glenelg Brochs, round stone dwellings from the 1st century AD, are also in the vicinity.

Aristocratic cooks
North of the Clan Donald Centre, on the coast, if the bank balance permits, you can have a meal cooked for you by the wife of the present clan chief. Together with her husband, Lady Claire Mac-Donald, who has written several successful Scottish cookery books, runs the exclusive Kinloch Lodge Hotel.

The Clan Donald Centre

SLEAT

The southeast of Skye consists of the peninsula of **Sleat** (pronounced Slate), the traditional lands of the MacDonalds. In the **Clan Donald Centre** (open Apr–Nov: daily from 9.30am) you can learn how the MacDonalds acquired the title 'Lords of the Isles' and then became the best organised clan of modern times. Its members come here from all over the world, particularly North America.

There is a beautiful walk at the southern end of the peninsula (from the chapel in Aird of Sleat, where the road ends, along the path on the other side of the gate to the lighthouse on the Point of Sleat – the journey there and back is around 5½ miles/9km).

Map
on pages
66–67

Romantic associations
Loch Coruisk has been immortalised by romantic painters and poets alike. In his epic poem, *The Lord of the Isles,* Walter Scott described it as a grim and gloomy place with a total absence of vegetation. This passage was illustrated by Turner with one of his most dramatic watercolours (*Loch Coruisk, Skye,* National Gallery of Scotland, Edinburgh). However, even these two eminent men should not be taken too literally: the lake is often bathed in sunshine and surrounded by a proliferation of flowering plants

THE CUILLINS

The road skirts Bla Bheinn, an impressive mountain with the famous ★★ **Cuillin Hills** as a backdrop, and continues to **Elgol**. At the end of the road, where it drops down to the shore, there is a car park off to the right. Take a deep breath as you get out of your car and give yourself time to absorb the spectacular view. In the foreground to the west is the little island of Soay, since 1953 no longer inhabited all the year round; to the south are the 'Small Isles' of Rum and Canna and to the northwest are the Cuillins. In the summer there are boat trips from Elgol quay across Loch Scavaig to the mountains opposite, with an opportunity to get out on the opposite shore and climb up to **Loch Coruisk**. Although (or maybe because) it is not easily accessible, this freshwater lake high up in the mountains has become one of the most famous views in Scotland.

Mountaineers can take the easier routes up the **Red Cuillins** from Sligachan Hotel on the A850, or venture up the awesome **Black Cuillins** from Glenbrittle – for experienced climbers only.

DUNVEGAN CASTLE

Below: the Red Cuillin Hills

On the other side of the Cuillins, follow the A863 along the southwest coast of Skye, with possible detours to the Talisker Whisky Distillery, the Colbost Folk Museum and the Piping Centre in Boreraig, which supplies information on almost everything worth knowing about bagpipes and their music. Eventually the road will bring you to ★ **Dunvegan Castle**, the ancestral seat of the Chief of the MacLeod clan (open Mar–Oct: daily 10am–5.30pm; Nov–Feb: on request, tel: 01470 521206). Of special interest are the exhibits from the time of the Jacobite Risings and the clan memorabilia, in particular the 'Fairy Flag'. According to legend the banner was given to the fourth chief by a fairy with whom he had fallen hopelessly in love. It has been unfurled twice to bring the fairy-folk to assist the clan in an emergency – it can only be used once more and then its power will be exhausted.

PORTREE

The main town on Skye is **Portree**. The picturesque rows of houses on the banks of the loch, with shops and bed and breakfast accommodation, might tempt you to stay here a little longer. Viewfield House, a hotel south of the town centre, is equally inviting – unless, that is, you are put off by stuffed animals and dinner round the large family table. Those interested in traditional music and dancing should not miss the folk festival at the end of July/beginning of August (information tel: 01471 844207), and should go to the Gathering Hall on a Friday evening (where joining in the dancing seems to be obligatory).

North of Portree, on the east coast of the peninsula of Trotternish off the A855, are a number of spectacular natural features. The first is the rather bizarre-looking **Old Man of Storr**, highest of a group of rocky pinnacles. It is possible to climb up to it from the car park, although the steep paths should be negotiated with some caution and stout shoes are necessary. The view to the south and east is magnificent.

LOCH MEALT

Further north is Loch Mealt, a small lake which sheds its water over the edge of the cliffs into the sea. From the edge of the road, Kilt Rock can be seen in the cliffs, with folds and patterns in

Star Attraction
● The Cuillins

Below: the Old Man of Storr
Bottom: Portree salmon

Map on pages 66–67

its strata said to resemble the Scottish national dress. And on the other side of the village of Staffin is a further collection of unusual rocks known as **Quiraing**. In order to examine them close up, turn off at Broraig on the road signposted Uig, which has a car park about 2½ miles (4km) further on. A short but quite strenuous walk will take you to the main group of rock formations, with names such as The Needle and The Table.

A hostel for backpackers, a pub with traditional music and dancing, and a more sophisticated hotel (Flodigarry Country House) may all be found in close proximity on the A855 north of Quiraing; locals, hotel guests and backpackers all join in the Saturday evening *ceilidh* in the pub.

Below: Flora MacDonald's house
Bottom: Skye Museum of Island Life exhibit

FLORA MACDONALD'S HOUSE

Also in the vicinity is a house once lived in by Flora MacDonald. Her name is associated with the romantic story of Bonnie Prince Charlie, the Young Pretender, who fled to the Hebrides after the crushing defeat of Culloden and was rescued by this courageous young woman.

Flora MacDonald is buried at **Kilmuir** on the western side of the Trotternish peninsula. The tall Celtic cross in the cemetery above the sea marks the spot where, in 1790, a huge crowd assembled at her funeral. Also at Kilmuir are the thatched cottages of the **Skye Museum of Island Life** (open Apr–Oct: Mon–Sat from 9am) which illustrates the lives of the rural population during different eras.

OUTER HEBRIDES

Uig is a small harbour south of Kilmuir, with a car ferry service that runs once or twice a day except on Sunday (the crossing takes 1¾ or 4 hours) between Uig (Skye), Lochmaddy (North Uist) and Tarbert (Harris). This will be a new experience: in the **Outer Hebrides** the local people often speak Gaelic among themselves, and in the schools the children are taught in both English and Gaelic. Church services on both the Protestant islands in the north and the Catholic islands in the south (the religious border runs through the island of Benbecula) are also usually held in Gaelic. On the double island of Lewis and Harris in particular, Sunday is still strictly observed as a day of rest – not only are the museums and shops shut, but also most pubs and petrol stations. A leaflet obtainable on the ferry or from the Tourist Information Centre *(see page 119)* will help you read the street names, which are all in Gaelic.

LEWIS

Thus equipped, head along the east coast of the double island (the southern tip is called Hearadh/ Harris, the larger northern part Leodhais/Lewis) to Steornabhagh/Stornoway, where the information centre will help with accommodation and general information for the whole of the Outer Hebrides. With a population of around 8,100, ★**Stornoway** is by far the largest place in these islands and thus has the best stocked shops and also has an airport. To learn more about the history of the region visit the **Museum nan Eilean/Western Isles Museum** in the Old Town Hall. Various exhibitions are shown in the **An Lanntair** cultural centre in the same building (open Mon–Sat 10am–5.30pm).

> **Flora MacDonald**
> Flora MacDonald risked her life for Bonnie Prince Charlie, but, like much connected with the Jacobite Risings, their flight was characterised by individual heroism, organisational chaos and political naivety in equal measure. Although she brought him from the Outer Hebrides to Skye, he thus missed the French ship that arrived at Benbecula three days later to collect him. When the prince finally reached France, John MacDonald of Borodale wrote bitterly: 'And that was how he went away from us, leaving us all in a worse state than he found us'. Flora MacDonald was arrested and imprisoned in the Tower of London; she later went to America but returned to Skye where she was honoured by her fellow Scots, and was highly regarded as a conversationalist.

Crab fishing on Harris

Map on pages 66–67

Harris tweed
The famous Harris tweed can only be sold as such if it has been woven on hand-looms on the Outer Hebrides from pure Scottish wool and bears the trade mark of the Harris Tweed Association.

ACROSS THE ISLAND

From Stornoway cross the moors to the northwest coast on the other side of the island. Here the road divides: turn right to reach the northernmost tip of the island, with its lighthouse, Rubha Robhanais/Butt of Lewis. With the sea on all sides there is a real sense of being in the middle of the Atlantic. Return to the road junction and continue southwest, past the **Black House Museum** in **Arnol** (open Mon–Sat from 10am). These 'black houses' were built without chimneys and heated with peat fires, the smoke escaping through the thatched roof.

Beautiful beaches (such as those at Dail Mor/Dalmore and Dail Beag/Dalbeg) are not all there is on offer; the clatter of looms can be heard from many houses – in Siabost/Shawbost and Carlabhagh/Carloway you can see tweed being made.

CALLANISH

One of the most important prehistoric sites in Europe is to be found at ★★ **Calanais/Callanish**. The stone circle, dominated by a huge menhir, with a burial cairn at the centre, and the rows of monoliths pointing outwards from the circle in the rough shape of a cross, has been described as 'a crowning achievement of the stone circle architects'. It is situated on a tongue

Calanais Standing Stones

of land jutting out into East Loch Roag, with an uninterrupted view of sea and sky. There is a good Visitors' Centre with souvenir shop and café nearby (open Apr–Sept: Mon–Sat 10am–7pm; Oct–Mar: 10am–4pm; stone circle all day).

Star Attractions
● Calanais
● Harris

HARRIS

At Gearraigh Na H-Aibhe/Garynahine take the B8011 to the south. The scenery, with its moors, rocks, pastures (called *machair* and typical of these islands) consisting of shell sand with many different kinds of wild flowers growing in it, and endless beaches pounded by the Atlantic, is worth savouring for a little longer. Spend a night at the Baile-Na-Cille hotel at Timsgarry, which is to be recommended for its idyllic location, child-oriented atmosphere and substantial Scottish fare.

Below: fishing off Harris
Bottom: Tarbert harbour

To reach the part of the island known as ★★ **Harris**, turn back to the main road. South of Tarbert the beaches on the west coast are even longer and more magnificent. In a climate warm enough for swimming they would be completely full, and there would be dozens of hotels here, of which none would be even half as enchanting or as good as Scarista House on the A895.

LEVERBURGH

On the south coast of Harris is **An T-ob/Lever-burgh**. The English name of the place is a reference to the large-scale experiment undertaken by the soap magnate Lord Leverhulme (Unilever) in the 1920s. After acquiring the double island in 1918–19 he began to modernise it by building a fishing harbour, buying trawlers and starting to build roads and fish-canneries. On the mainland he opened his own chain of fish shops (called MacFisheries) to sell the catch. He also had plans to rationalize fishing with the latest technology, including the use of planes to search for shoals of herrings. The local population were at first slow to respond to his enthusiasm for development, but were gradually won over by the employment possibilities that were being offered.

Outside the Polachar Inn, South Uist

In 1923 Lord Leverhulme was obliged to let his plans for Lewis drop. Although he continued to invest generously in Harris and Leverburgh, when he died in 1925 his legal heirs stopped all payments. The harbour of Leverburgh, however, remains as a testimony to this grandiose project.

NORTH UIST

There is a car ferry from Leverburgh to Otternish on **Uibhist A Tuath/North Uist** (Mon–Sat 3–4 times daily, crossing time 1 hour 10 minutes). Those who prefer even lonelier places can cross from Otternish to the small island of Bhearnaraigh/Berneray. North Uist and the isles to the south, Beinn Na Faoghla/Benbecula and Uibhist A Deas/South Uist, together form a long strip of land connected by embankments. The east coast is rocky, with large bays and small offshore islands, while the western coastline consists primarily of long sandy beaches between promontories. Machair pastures are typical of the interior.

On North Uist, the **sanctuary** at **Baile Raghaill/Balranald** is particularly recommended for birdwatchers (those interested should report to the supervisor). It covers an area of 1,626 acres (658 hectares) and has a wide range of habitats: salt water, rocks, sandy beaches, dunes, *machair*, marsh and freshwater, so it is scarcely surprising that 183 species of bird have been seen here, 50 of which breed in the sanctuary every year.

Also on the island is a well-preserved prehistoric site; the burial cairn of Bharpa Langais/Barpa Langass (on the road from Lochmaddy to Clachan), dates from around 1000BC and is said to be the burial place of a person of high standing in the society.

SOUTH UIST

On **Benbecula**, the legacy of the former army presence is a large housing estate – not exactly a feast for the eyes. At least the inhabitants have unusually good shopping facilities and an airport which is used by civilian aircraft from Glasgow.

★ **South Uist** is around 20 miles (32 km) long, but only just over 6 miles (10km) across at its widest point. From Loch Baghasdail/Lochboisdale in the southern part of the island, there is a ferry to Barra or Mallaig/Oban on the mainland (Tues, Thur, Fri and Sun, crossing time to Barra is 1½ hours, to Mallaig/Oban 7–9 hours). The west coast is renowned for its long, sandy beaches, and the eastern part of the island is dominated by the impressive **Ben More** (2,000ft/610m). The views from the summit are quite magnificent but the walk to reach it is long and tortuous.

If time and weather permit, go right to the southern tip of South Uist and sit outside the Polachar Inn to watch the long drawn-out sunset against a backdrop of islands in the south and the endless Atlantic in the west.

BARRA

★★ **Eilean Bharraigh/Barra** is a particularly charming and friendly place. The main village, Bagh a Chaistail/Castlebay, has a harbour with a castle in the middle of it (Kisimul Castle dating from the 13th century), and there is a lively pub, the Castlebay Bar, near the hotel of the same name. Depending on the season, it may be possible to see the large colony of seals in Seal Bay (information in the Tourist Information Centre).

Star Attraction
● Barra

Beach landing
The famous airstrip on the shell beach of **Traigh Mhor** on Barra, which can be used only when the tide is out, is frequently rumoured to be in line for improvement (which seems to be a euphemism for concreted over), but until then the flight from Glasgow will remain one of the most exciting of any made by a scheduled airline.

Island transport

Map
on page
92

*Below: sorting the
catch on Mull
Bottom: Ben Nevis*

8: The West

Lochaber – Argyll – The Southern Islands

The history of united, Christian Scotland began in the province of Dalriada in what is now Argyll, which was settled by Irish Scots. The Irish monk Columba landed here in the southwest in AD563, and founded the monastery on Iona that became the mother church of Celtic Christianity in Scotland. From Iona, monks were sent to convert the heathens on the mainland. This was the domain of the Scots king Kenneth MacAlpin, who defeated the Picts, joined his kingdom to theirs and gave the Scots their present name.

SCENERY

The route through Lochaber and Argyll leads first onto the Isle of Mull from Oban, and from there north through the beautiful scenery of the peninsulas of Morvern, Ardnamurchan and Moidart to Fort William. It then runs south through Glencoe, and follows Loch Awe to the peninsula of Kintyre, with a detour to the islands of Islay and Jura, both famed for their whisky.

The geography of this area means you will spend almost as much time on ferries as on the road, with the added bonus that the views of the countryside from the sea are quite breathtaking.

OBAN

Oban could be called the gateway to the Hebrides. This is the departure point for the ferries to Mull, Barra, South Uist and Colonsay and the nearby islands of Kerrera and Lismore, and the town is the tourist centre for the whole county of Argyll. Every August the **Argyllshire Highland Gathering** is held in Oban, with folk music and traditional dancing. The town is not only a focal point for holidaymakers but also the shopping centre for the rural population of the entire region, so that even outside the main season Oban always seems very busy.

MCCAIG'S TOWER

The unusual building, called McCaig's Tower, perched on the hill immediately behind the harbour, may, with a little imagination, remind you of the Colosseum in Rome; at least this was the intention of its designer. The banker John Stuart McCaig, who was a great admirer of Roman art and architecture, had the building erected between 1890 and 1900, partly to provide a source of employment for the local population, but finally he could no longer afford (or was no longer prepared to pay for) the project, as costs rose steeply. So the tower was never completed – hence its other name, McCaig's Folly. The view over the loch to Mull and the smaller islands makes the ascent worthwhile.

The best hotel in Oban is on the coast road south of the town centre. Called the Manor House, it has a high reputation, especially for its cuisine.

LOCH LINNHE

A visit to the island of **Lismore** in **Loch Linnhe** is particularly recommended (a ferry from Oban runs 4–5 times daily except Sun; approximately 50-minute crossing time; a ferry from Port Appin maintains a continuous service daily until 7pm; approximately 10-minute crossing time, only for pedestrians and cyclists). Points of interest on the island are a round tower *(broch)* dating from the

A long line of visitors
The long inlets which divide the land up into peninsulas and offshore islands have attracted visitors since prehistoric times, many of whom established themselves in the area. Today, following in the footsteps of the Irish Celts and Vikings, the visitors are tourists making pilgrimages to Iona, sailing on the lochs or attending the Argyllshire Highland Gathering in Oban in August.

Oban harbour and McCaig's Tower

ROUTE 8 THE WEST

0 _____ 30 km

0 _____ 20 miles

1st century AD at Tirefour, and the ruins of **Achadun Castle**, a former bishop's palace – the island was the seat of the diocese of Argyll from 1200 to 1507, and the ruins of the former cathedral can also be visited.

Map opposite

MULL

The other island that can be easily reached from Oban is ★ **Mull**, after Skye the second most accessible Inner Hebridean island (a car ferry to Craignure runs 6–8 times daily, Mon–Sat, 3–5 times daily on Sun, and connects with the train to Glasgow; the crossing takes approximately 40 minutes). The ferry passes close to a promontory dominated by the imposing **Duart Castle**. With a few interruptions this castle has been the seat of the chiefs of the MacLean clan since the 14th century, and is worth a visit (open May–Oct: daily 10.30am–6pm).

Railway buffs will enjoy a ride on the narrow-gauge line from the nearby pier in Craignure to **Torosay Castle**, 1½ miles (2½km) away. The castle (open Easter–mid-Oct: daily from 10.30am; garden all year) was built in 1856 and has attractive gardens.

The main town on Mull is ★ **Tobermory**, one of the settlements which were built more or less overnight in the 18th century by the British Fisheries Society. The brightly-coloured facades of the houses along the shore are a popular subject for photographers, and they lend the town its cheerful character. Strongarbh House, a Victorian villa on the hill behind the harbour, has a pleasant restaurant and also four rooms for overnight guests.

From Tobermory the single-track B8073 curves round to the southwest, never far away from the coast. After numerous twists and turns with lovely and constantly changing views (e.g. of Ben More, the highest mountain on Mull, and the offshore island of Ulva), it joins the road that leads westwards to **Fionnphort**. From here there is a 5-minute ferry crossing (pedestrians only, no vehicles) to Iona.

A grisly tale

The first Christian community on the island of Lismore is said to have been founded here in the 6th century by the Irish St Moluag. According to legend, he took part in a race to the island with St Columba: when Columba's boat took the lead near the shore, Moluag is said to have cut off one of his fingers and thrown it on the island in order to claim it for himself.

Colourful Tobermory

Map on page 92

Staffa excursion
From the quay in Iona (and from Oban) there are also boat trips to the little island of ★★ Staffa, with its imposing basalt columns and Fingal's Cave, which inspired Mendelssohn to write his *Hebrides Overture* (also called *Fingal's Cave*).

Celtic cross, Iona

IONA

The island of ★★ **Iona** is the cradle of Scottish Christianity. This is where, in 563, Columba came with his Irish monks to convert the Picts. In subsequent centuries the Vikings invaded the island a number of times, but it was only when Catholic property was expropriated in the 16th century that the monastery ceased to exist.

Of the remaining buildings, the **cathedral**, dating from 1500, is by far the largest. Also on the site are the ruins of an early-13th-century convent and smaller chapels. Most of these buildings were in a state of considerable disrepair at the beginning of this century; their restoration was the work of the Iona Community, founded by Dr George Macleod in 1938. The cemetery has great significance for the Scots. Until the 11th century it was the burial place of the Scottish kings, and, in addition to seven Norwegian and four Irish kings, there are said to be 48 Scottish rulers buried here, including Duncan, who was murdered by Macbeth. In Shakespeare's play, Rosse asks 'Where is Duncan's body?' and Macduff replies, 'Carried to Colmekill [Icolmkill or Iona]; The sacred storehouse of his predecessors/And guardian of their bones'. The cemetery is also the last resting place of John Smith, the much respected politician and leader of Britain's Labour Party from 1992 until his death in 1994.

Iona, or rather the monastery complex, is completely overrun with visitors in the summer. If you can manage it, therefore, it is advisable to take the first morning ferry (usually 8.45am, but check the exact time in advance) or even spend the night here, perhaps in the recommended Argyll Hotel, in order to enjoy the special atmosphere of the place at leisure.

MINING VILLAGE

From Fishnish in the northeastern part of Mull there is a ferry service to Lochaline on the peninsula of Morvern (Mon–Sat, every 50 minutes during the day, Sun every hour; crossing time approximately 15 minutes). From here, drive north through the highland valleys of Morvern to Loch Sunart, and then west along its northern shore to **Strontian**, the first place of any size along this road. It is not by chance that its name puts one in mind of radioactive isotopes: in the 18th century a new mineral was discovered in the lead mines here which was named strontianite, and the element strontium was isolated from it. The last lead mine was closed early in the 20th century, but a few new seams have recently been opened and the barite required for oil drilling in the North Sea is now being mined here.

Star Attractions
- Iona
- Staffa

Below: the shore at Strontian
Bottom: dramatic basalt on Staffa

ARDNAMURCHAN

Still on the shore of Loch Sunart, the road now takes you onto the elongated peninsula of **Ardnamurchan**. Those familiar with this part of Scotland will be aware that one of the main attractions of this peninsula – at least for those who could afford it – was the Glenborrodale Castle Hotel, once one of the plushest hotels in Scotland. The impressive Victorian pile has been sold, however, and turned into a private home and can no longer be visited.

But the peninsula still has one particular treat that is worth the long drive to reach it: **Sanna Bay**. From the car park in Sanna it is possible to walk south along the coast, with its sandy beaches and

Map on page 92

small bays between rocky promontories and dunes, to Portuairk. It is just under 2 miles (3km) there and back, and is quite an easy stroll, except that there is no clearly visible path. The numerous stationary caravans that are used by the people of the region as holiday homes do rather spoil the scenery, but they are one way of having a cheap holiday in this area.

CASTLE TIORAM

To the north of the Ardnamurchan peninsula, the 14th-century ★ **Castle Tioram** is lapped by the tides of the little Loch Moidart. At ebb tide, stranded on the gleaming mud, it looks as if it were washed up there centuries ago, while at high tide it towers majestically out of the water. Its position provides ample explanation why it could never be taken – it was partially destroyed for the first time in only 1715 when the lord of the castle himself set fire to it to prevent it falling into the hands of the Campbells, while he and his men were off fighting for the Jacobite cause.

Loch nan Uamh is also associated with the 18th-century Jacobites; this was where, in July 1745, Bonnie Prince Charlie disembarked from a French brig in order to raise the standard at Glenfinnan. The memorial column at the point where the splendid **Loch Shiel** opens to view, is crowned

The Ben

Fort William is the starting point for the walk to the top of the highest mountain in Great Britain, ★★ Ben Nevis (4,406ft/ 1343m). The car parks at the foot of wide, well-trodden paths should not deceive you into thinking that this is an easy mountain to climb: it should only be tackled with the proper equipment since it is a hike of 11 miles (18km) there and back and the weather is notoriously unreliable. In the main season the long line of people tramping up may make the expedition seem more like a penance than an adventure, but the view makes an overwhelming impression on everyone who has stood on the summit in fine weather.

The Glenfinnan memorial

by the figure of a Highland warrior, not, as is often thought, the prince himself. It was put up in 1815 by MacDonald of Glenaladale, whose ancestor had marched over the hill with the men of his clan, just as the prince feared he had been abandoned by all but a few faithful supporters.

The subsequent fate of the region is revealed by the fact that in 1745 the valley of Glenaladale was able to send 100 men into battle whereas now it is completely uninhabited. In September 1746, a second French ship entered Loch nan Uamh to take the defeated Charles on board and get him out of the country. After this the government troops were once more firmly in charge of the country.

FORT WILLIAM

The garrison of the government troops in **Fort William** held out against the rebellions of 1715 and 1745. The fort no longer exists and the town is now exposed to invasions of tourists.

The history of the region is well illustrated in the ★ **West Highland Museum** (open June–Sept: Mon–Sat 10am–5pm; July and Aug: Sun 2–5pm; Oct–May: Mon–Sat 10am–4pm). Fort William is the regional centre of Lochaber and a key tourist centre: it is the most important stop on the railway line from Glasgow to Mallaig (at certain periods the train is pulled by a steam engine on the beautiful stretch to the west coast); and it is the junction of the main roads from the Grampians, Inverness and the northwest (Skye and Wester Ross).

GLENCOE

South of Fort William, on the other side of the bridge at Ballachulish, is the village of Glencoe, at the entrance to the valley of ★★★ **Glencoe**, one of the most impressive, dramatic and romantic places in all of Scotland. The car parks, campsites and visitors' centre, etc. do not detract in the slightest from the overwhelming majesty of the glen. The steeply rising road winds between rock walls that gradually close in until, at the top end of the glen, it comes out onto the open plateau

Below: Fort William
Bottom: a Glencoe mountainside

Map on page 92

The Glencoe massacre
In February 1692, Robert Campbell of Glenlyon arrived with his troops in Glencoe and invented a pretext to ask the resident MacDonalds for accommodation. The government in London had given orders that this powerful, rebellious Highland clan must be taught a lesson, and thus one morning Campbell's soldiers suddenly turned on the valley's inhabitants, killing 38 who were unable to flee with their families into the mountains. The Massacre of Glencoe created a great deal of bad blood between the MacDonalds and Campbells and increased the clans' mistrust of the central government – many Highlanders also interpreted the Jacobite Risings which took place 23 years later as revenge for Glencoe.

of **Rannoch Moor**. One of the main attractions of Glencoe for mountaineers is the famous ridge walk over **Aonach Eagach**. This narrow, exposed ridge should be attempted only by experienced climbers and is certainly not something for anyone who is afraid of heights. Running roughly south from Glencoe is the beautiful Glen Etive, also famous for its climbing.

However, many less adventurous visitors come to the valley to see the location of a notorious episode in Scottish history *(see panel)*. In the **Visitor Centre** (open May–Aug: daily 9.30am–5.30pm; Apr, Sept and Oct: 10am–5pm), an exhibition which makes the most of modern technology explains the events that took place.

INVERARAY

After Bridge of Orchy take the B8074 in the direction of Dalmally and Loch Awe. At the north end of **Loch Awe** is the impressive ruin of ★ **Kilchurn Castle**. To reach Ardanasaig Hotel near **Kilchrenan** for an overnight stay, it is necessary to round the end of the loch and drive some distance along single-track roads to the west shore, but the detour is well worthwhile. The manor house, built in 1834, is surrounded by beautiful gardens and not only has extremely attractive rooms but also excellent food.

Glen Etive

On the northwest shore of Loch Fyne is **Inveraray**. This attractive place, dating from the 18th century, is totally reliant on tourists, who are primarily attracted by the castle. The seat of the Duke of Argyll and chief of the Campbell clan, it was built at the same time as Inveraray itself and has a collection of paintings including works by Gainsborough, Ramsay and Raeburn, and lavishly decorated rooms with porcelain, furniture, tapestries and other treasures (open July and Aug: Mon–Sat 10am–5pm, Sun 1–5pm; Apr–June, Sept and Oct: Mon–Sat 10am–12.30pm and 2–5pm, Sun 2–5pm).

Below: Inverarary Castle
Bottom: charming Islay

AUCHINDRAIN

Although the **Argyll Wildlife Park** south of Inverary on the A83 (daily from 10am) is basically a zoo, it mainly has animals native to Scotland, kept in the most natural surroundings possible. There are sheep and chickens wandering around freely, which are particularly popular with children. **Auchindrain** is a Highland village which has been prevented from falling into ruin and been partially restored to give tourists an idea of traditional life in the Highlands (**Auchindrain Township Open Air Museum**, open Apr–Sept: daily 10am– 5pm). Further south on the shore of the loch is **Crarae Garden** (opening uncertain at present). There are three marked paths through the woodlands, with their waterfalls and azaleas, eucalyptus trees and rhododendrons, for which the park is famous. The shortest of these walks takes about 45 minutes.

ISLAY

Further along the magnificent loch shore, bear south via Lochgilphead and Tarbert/Knapdale to the elongated peninsula of **Kintyre**. From Kennacraig there is a ferry to ★ **Islay** (1–3 times a day; the crossing to Port Ellen takes 2 hours and to Port Askaig 1¾ hours).

The **distilleries** of **Laphroaig** and **Lagavulin** at Port Ellen are open to visitors – the free tastes

Map
on page
92

Islay malts
The malts of Islay are well known for their peaty flavour; this is derived from the drying of the barley in peat-fired kilns. The Islay peat contains a high proportion of heather and seaweed, which further adds to the whisky's distinctive taste.

Whisky in the making

of these two whiskies are enough by themselves to make the trip to Islay worthwhile. A small turning off on the main road to Bowmore leads to Kintra, which has a beautifully located campsite, a good pub/hotel nearby and 5 miles (8km) of magnificent sandy beach.

The golf course on the dunes is said by those in the know to be a particular challenge. There is also a civilian airfield here, but you will seldom be disturbed by it (it is primarily used by golfers making quick trips from Glasgow).

In the west of Islay on the peninsula called the **Rhinns of Islay** is Port Charlotte, a pretty place where you can visit the **Museum of Islay Life**; there is excellent bed and breakfast accommodation to be had in some of the houses along the shore road.

Islay has many fascinating prehistoric and ancient sites, including the stone circle of Cultoon in the southern part of Rhinns, which it is assumed was never completed. It is thought that the stones lying on the ground did not fall over but were brought to the spot and then never set upright. The island has several well-preserved Celtic crosses, one of which may be found at the church of Kilchoman.

JURA

From Port Askaig in the northeast there is a ferry to the island of **Jura** (continuous services during the day except Sun; the crossing takes 10 minutes): it is the only way to reach this island. The only road here circles the impressive Paps of Jura, with its hunting areas, and winds along the east coast in a northerly direction. This fairly large island (28 miles/45km long and 8 miles/13km across at its widest point) seems to have nobody on it but tourists.

In 1947–8 George Orwell came here to work on his novel *1984* and lived at Barnhill, a completely isolated farmhouse in the northern part of the island. The house is not accessible to the public, and the walk too strenuous to make it feasible for most people, even to go and look at it from the outside. Orwell himself described it as being quite easy to reach, if it were not for the fact that the last 8 miles (13km) had to be covered on foot.

THE MULL OF KINTYRE

After returning to Kintyre on the mainland, you can either drive south as far as Campbeltown and the **Mull of Kintyre**, at the tip of the peninsula (which is only 12½ miles (20km) away from Northern Ireland), or go in an easterly direction straight across the peninsula to Claonaig, where there is a ferry to Lochranza on Arran, and finally return to the mainland quite close to Glasgow.

ARRAN AND BUTE

The islands of **Arran** and **Bute** in the Firth of Clyde are extremely popular with Glaswegians. The largest places here (Brodick on Arran, Rothesay on Bute) and the popular beaches become very full during the summer holidays, at weekends and on public holidays, but the beautiful scenery away from the main roads, especially the ridge leading to the 2,866-foot (874-metre) peak of Goatfell, is more than adequate compensation for the queues at the ferries.

Below: Goatfell, Arran
Bottom: mountain, moor and sea

MARIA
D   G
SCOTIÆ
ISSIMA REGINA
ANCIÆ DOTARIA
ANNO
ÆTATIS REGNIQ
36
ANGLICÆ CAPTIVIT
10
S   H
1578

Art History

PAINTING AND SCULPTURE

The culture of the Picts has survived solely in the form of metal objects and sculpted stone. The style with which these objects were decorated (with symbols and images of animals) was at first quite distinct from the more ornamental work of the Scots who emigrated from Ireland, but the two styles later blended. Most of the illuminated books and medieval church ornamentation were lost when the monasteries were destroyed in the 16th century – only a few isolated examples remain, which illustrate just how closely the style of the medieval artists in Scotland was connected with that of their counterparts on the European continent. The same is true of court painting, which, until the 17th century, was primarily the province of Flemish and Dutch artists. An independent Scottish movement developed in the second half of the 16th century, which was reflected in richly decorated room ceilings (Crathes Castle).

With the flowering of the 'Scottish Enlightenment', the 18th century became the era of great portrait painting (Allan Ramsay: *Margaret Lindsay*, Henry Raeburn: *Macdonell of Glengarry*). Both are in the National Gallery of Scotland (NGS), Edinburgh, which provides a good overall survey of Scotland's fine arts. Landscape artists such as Alexander Runciman and Alexander Nasmyth were still wedded to the classical ideal: Greece, Rome and peaceful Lowland landscapes were their subject matter. It was not until the 19th century that the romantic transformation of the Highlands began to be reflected in painting, in, for example, the dramatic genre scenes of David Wilkie (*Distraining for Rent*, NGS) and the glowering landscapes of Horatio McCulloch.

The modern age was heralded by William McTaggert. He began as a genre painter, but his large-scale seascapes, painted at the end of the 19th century (*The Sailing of the Emigrant Ship*, NGS), give an entirely personal impression of the environment. The group of painters known as the Glasgow Boys (including James Guthrie: *A*

> **Contemporary art**
> Amongst the artists who are active in Scotland today, John Bellany is particularly well known for his portraits, and Ian Hamilton Finlay for his sculptures. The artists who call themselves the Edinburgh Girls (June Redfern, Fionna Carlisle), cultivate an expressive, figurative style; and Ken Currie, born in 1960, has made a name for himself with his dramatic murals for the Glasgow People's Palace.

Opposite: Mary Queen of Scots
Below: Pictish inscription, Inverarary
Bottom: 'The Painter's Wife' by Ramsay

Scottish neoclassicism
In 1700 the splendid age of Scottish neoclassicism was introduced by the architect Colin Campbell, following in the footsteps of Andrea Palladio. The most outstanding representatives of this era were Robert and James Adam, the creators of Charlotte Square in Edinburgh, Hopetoun House, and Culzean Castle with its incredible combination of neoclassical elements and romantic castle architecture. The Adams planned every interior down to the tiniest decorative detail.

Hind's Daughter; W.Y. Macgregor: *The Vegetable Stall*; both in the NGS) was strongly influenced by French Impressionism, as was S.J. Peploe who spearheaded the 'colourist' movement at the beginning of the 20th century.

ARCHITECTURE AND DESIGN

The fact that a building has been put up in Scotland by no means classifies it as 'Scottish architecture'. In the long history of Scottish architecture not only most of the ideas, but also most of the architects, came from the European continent or England. On the other hand, Scotland did produce several architects whose influence spread not only to England, but elsewhere in Europe and beyond.

The beginning of the 14th century saw the development of a specifically Scottish type of fortified complex: the tower house, a massive tower with a kitchen and stables on the ground floor, large hall on the first floor and private apartments above it (Threave Castle, Dumfries and Galloway; Drum Castle, Grampian).

In the 19th century this elegant simplicity was largely abandoned in favour of the pompous style beloved by Victorian architects, whose monumental buildings, with their plethora of ornamentation, suitably reflected the commercial pride of their municipal clients (City Chambers, Glasgow).

Glasgow City Chambers

The counter-movement, known as the 'Glasgow Style', introduced an independent form of art nouveau architecture: under the leadership of Charles Rennie Mackintosh, this group of architects specialised in clear forms and geometric decoration – buildings such as the Glasgow School of Art or Hill House in Helensburgh, with their highly unusual combination of tradition and modernity, are among the most original in the history of Scottish architecture. Here, too, the interior design of a building was considered to be as important as the exterior.

Below: Mackintosh's Glasgow School of Art
Bottom: bust of Burns

LITERATURE

Scottish literature has been written in three different languages. While for a long time only the literature in English was taken seriously, more recently the texts in Scots dialect and Gaelic have been receiving increasing attention. Literature written in the vernacular began to be circulated in 1350, and by 1375 the great Scottish national epic, John Barbour's rhyming chronicle, *The Bruce*, had appeared in the English dialect of the Scottish Lowlands. In around 1500, poets such as Robert Henryson and William Dunbar were producing celebrated verse allegories and satires, and the cleric Gavin Douglas's rendering of Virgil's *Aeneid* was one of the first versions of classical literature to appear in English.

Around 1725, with pastorals such as *The Gentle Shepherd* by Allan Ramsay and James Thomson's *The Seasons* (set to music by Haydn), Scottish literature began to spread throughout Europe. James Macpherson's fabricated 'Transcriptions' of the Ossian poems were published in 1765: the schoolmaster collected Gaelic ballads, which he translated, summarised and published with a faked historical classification as an original Gaelic epic entitled *Fingal*. This sensational 'finding' was the talk of Europe. *Fingal* became the favourite work of many Romantics, who also admired the poems of Robert Burns and Walter Scott. Scott's historical novels *(Waverley, Ivanhoe, Quentin Durward)* were best-sellers

Below: *Sir Walter Scott*
Below: *R.L. Stevenson*

in the early 19th century, while Burns' dialect poems earned him the title 'Scottish national poet'. In the mid-19th century Thomas Carlyle contributed significantly to the cultural life of the Victorian age with his historical studies and polemics. Towards the end of the century came Robert Louis Stevenson who penned such famous tales as *Treasure Island*, *Kidnapped* and *Dr Jekyl and Mr Hyde*.

Gaelic literature first became known to a wider public during the Romantic age, when the oral productions of the story-teller Rob Donn MacAoidh (Robert MacKay) and the lyric poet Donnchadh Ban Mac an t-Saoir (Duncan Ban MacIntyre), whose work is characterised by themes from nature, were written down, translated into English and published. Alasdair Mac Mhaighstir Alasdair (Alexander MacDonald), born in 1695, is considered to be the greatest of the literary Gaelic poets.

The 20th century brought a revival of Scottish lyric poetry, both in English (Hugh MacDiarmid: *A Drunk Man Looks at the Thistle*) and Gaelic (Somhairle MacGill-Eain/Sorley Maclean), while Scottish novelists continue to make a significant impact on English literature: famous names include Alasdair Gray *(Lanark)*, Iain Banks *(The Wasp Factory, The Crow Road)*, A.L. Kennedy *(Now That You're Back),* Irvine Welsh, whose first novel, *Trainspotting*, hit the headlines in 1993 and was made into a successful film and play, and James Kelman, who won the Booker prize in 1994 with *How Late It Was, How Late*.

MUSIC

To most people the term 'Scottish music' means folk music, or more precisely the bagpipes or the amplified instruments of the folk revival. Even well-informed classical music-lovers would probably be hard put to come up immediately with the name of a Scottish composer. But since the time of the Celtic bards and the medieval Roman-Catholic monks, Scotland has had a tradition of great musicians whose names are now quite unknown: the five masses and two motets composed by the Catholic church musician Robert Carver (born in 1485) rank highly, in the opinion of the experts, among contemporary European compositions, although until recently there was no complete edition of Carver's opus. The virtuoso consort music of Tobias Hume (born in 1569) and the airs of John Abell (born in around 1652), who toured France, Italy and Germany as a famous singer, are equally unknown.

In the 18th and 19th centuries there was a dominant Italian influence in Scottish music, but composers such as James Oswald (born in 1711) also collected folk tunes and preserved them for posterity, while folk music instrumentalists, such as the famous fiddler Niel Gow, played at the courts of the nobility, where the traditional dances became well-known. These melodies thus found their way to continental Europe, and ultimately resurfaced in the 'Scottish' music of Haydn, Beethoven, L.A. Kozeluch, Weber, Mendlessohn-Bartholdy and many others.

TRADITIONAL MUSIC

Scotland's famous folk music has an equally long tradition. Carvings of harps have been found on 8th-century picture stones: as the first national instrument of Scotland, the harp was played at the courts of the Picts. Today the Scottish Celtic harp

Contemporary music
The 20th century saw the transition from imitations of European conventional music to modern music acknowledged the world over, from John Blackwood McEwen's impressionistic portrayals of the landscape *(Under Northern Skies)* to the 'dramatic and abstract' forms of Thea Musgrave, and the latest international successes of Judith Weir *(A Night at the Chinese Opera)* and James MacMillan.

Church choir

Traditional revival
The modern folk revival involves a mixture of styles. Alongside the pipes, fiddles, flutes and accordions, groups such as Battlefield Band, Capercaillie, Ceolbeg, Tannahill Weavers and Wolfstone also employ rock-music instruments in their repertoires. More traditional forms of music are provided by singers such as Cilla Fisher and Christine Primrose, the harpist Alison Kinnaird, the fiddler Ali Bain or the lowland piper Hamish Moore – to name but a few of the musicians who regularly perform at the countless concerts and festivals that take place up and down the country.

or *clarsach*, a harp without pedals and tuned diatonically, is again becoming increasingly popular.

The bagpipes, which originally supplanted the harp, were probably introduced from Southern Europe as a pastoral and festive instrument. In around 1600, a complex repertory was developed with a hierarchy of music beginning with the 'small music' *(ceòl beag)*, consisting of jigs and reels, etc., followed by the 'middle music' *(ceòl meadhonach)* consisting of slow airs and laments, and finally the 'great music' or pibroch *(ceòl mór)*, basically variations on a theme, which has been handed down through generations of piping families. The military use of bagpipes with drums dates from the 18th century.

Of the various kinds of bagpipes originally found in Scotland, the Scottish Highland bagpipe is the one most commonly played today, although the Scottish Lowland bagpipe, originally played from about 1750 to 1850, is also heard a great deal; like the Irish Uillean pipes, this instrument is bellows-blown.

The other national instrument of Scotland is the fiddle, which also has a long tradition but became particularly popular in the 18th century; the Shetland Islands have their own repertoire and technique of playing. Latterly, the fiddle has been largely displaced by the piano accordion for the accompaniment of dancing.

A modern harp in a historic interior

Festivals

EDINBURGH

Every year for three weeks, from the middle of August to the beginning of September, Edinburgh explodes into life as it hosts one of the greatest music and theatre festivals in the world, the **International Festival of Music and Drama** (The Hub, Castlehill, Edinburgh EH1 2NE, tel: 0131 473 2000, e-mail: info@eif.co.uk). Every concert hall, basement theatre and church hall in the centre of the city overflows with dance groups, theatre companies, string quartets, opera companies and orchestras, and the streets are awash with fire eaters, jugglers, bagpipers, clowns, satirists and theatrical hopefuls of every shape, size and colour.

At the same time there are performances by numerous self-financing theatre groups, comedians and mime artists, collectively known as the **Festival Fringe** (180 High Street, EH1 1QS, tel: 0131 226 5257), which has now grown so big that it is in danger of outgrowing the city.

Also in August are the **International Film Festival** (88 Lothian Road, EH3 9BZ, tel: 0131 229 2550); the **International Jazz Festival** (116 The Canongate, EH8 8DD, tel: 0131 557 1642); and, biannually in 2003, 2005, 2007 etc, the **Book Festival** (137 Dundee Street, EH11 1BG, tel: 0131 225 5444).

Below: a symbol of Scotland
Bottom: Edinburgh Festival Fringe Theatre

GLASGOW

Until recently, Glasgow held its annual Mayfest, an attempt to provide an equivalent to the Edinburgh Festival. However, the popular event has been abandoned because of its high costs.

In July there is the **International Jazz Festival** (tel: 0141 552 3552), which attracts a host of famous names from the world of jazz, and also highlights Scottish talent, such as the saxophonist Tommy Smith. In January the much-acclaimed **Celtic Connections** festival of music comes to the Glasgow Royal Concert Hall (tel: 0141 353 8000). For information on further events call the TIC (tel: 0141 204 4400).

To Days
Specials

~~Cooked PRAWNS~~
~~PATE (SALMON & TROUT)~~
~~SCALLOP MEAT~~
SMOKED SALMON
FRESH SALMON
SCALLOP MEAT
MONK TAILS
FRESH TROUT
&
all kinds of white
& SMOKED FISH.

FOOD AND DRINK

Anyone who has ever eaten a traditional Burns' Night supper of haggis, potatoes and mashed swede, could be forgiven for thinking that Scottish cuisine was unimaginative and not very healthy. This was probably true in Burns' day, but the culinary scene in Scotland is now a lot more varied.

For good cuisine you must of course have good ingredients, and there is certainly no shortage of these in Scotland. The sea, rivers and lochs supply salmon and trout (fish caught in the wild are more expensive but also tastier than those from fish farms) and many other kinds of fish, plus mussels, scallops, crabs and lobsters fresh from the cutter.

Scotland is rightly famous for its lean beef and lamb – the animals are reared in natural conditions, grazing in the open – and this usually tastes best when prepared simply; venison and game birds are also typical dishes. Potatoes, cabbage, carrots and leeks are the traditional vegetables – and wild mushrooms have now also come into their own. Fruit-growing has a long tradition in the Lowlands, especially the cultivation of berries, and the produce is processed to make desserts and jams.

Oats occupy a special place in the Scottish diet. In 1775 Samuel Johnson famously defined them in his dictionary of the English language as 'a cereal which in England is generally fed to the horses, and in Scotland is eaten by the people'. Oats thrive in colder climates than other cereals, and as a result of the longer ripening process have a higher oil and protein content, so that they are extremely suitable as a basic nutrient for Scottish latitudes. Oatmeal is used to make unsweetened cakes (oatcakes, bannocks), porridge, brose and cloutie dumplings. To make the national dish of haggis, oatmeal is added to lamb offal (heart, lights and liver) which is cooked in the lining of a sheep's stomach (it tastes better than it sounds). Coarsely ground oats are also used to make caboc, which is oat-rolled cheese. Visitors who don't fancy the haggis may like to try some atholl brose: thin porridge mixed with honey and whisky.

Honey and whisky are also added to cranachan, which is basically a dessert consisting of toasted oatmeal, fruit and cream. The Scots are known for having a sweet tooth: in the 18th century they were still mainly using honey as a sweetener (and still maintain that their heather honey is the best in the world), but today their sugar consumption is higher than elsewhere in Britain. Their shortbread (shortcake pastry biscuits) is famous all over the world, with its simple recipe known to every schoolchild as 'six, four, two': six parts of flour, four parts of butter and two parts of sugar.

Big breakfasts

A Scottish breakfast may consist not only of the usual egg, bacon and tomato plus toast, but also of mushrooms, sausages, smoked fish, porridge, black pudding, fried potatoes, and kidneys in brown sauce. This is accompanied by tea, usually made from tea bags (except in the very best hotels or some private homes), or coffee, which the Scots nowadays often prefer to tea, and which can be of very good quality. But strong tea with milk and sugar is still regarded as the universal remedy for any kind of shock.

Opposite: a Portree menu

Scottish pubs are no longer the exclusively male preserves they used to be. They serve the usual soft drinks and local mineral water, in addition to various kinds of beer. Many pubs in Scotland now sell 'real ale', cask-conditioned beer in various strengths (60°, 70° and 80°) made by Scottish brewers – ask for 80-shilling rather than 'heavy'. Caledonian 70-shilling and 80-shilling are traditionally made in a Victorian Edinburgh brewery.

Scotch whisky is exploited for all it's worth by the tourist trade, and there are numerous distilleries which can be visited *(see pages 63 and 100)*. Scotch is roughly divided into the commoner grain whisky, and the expensive, unblended single malt, produced solely from malted barley and cellared in oak vats for at least eight years.

Restaurants

The Scottish Tourist Board, and associated tourist organisations, have produced a guide to the country's restaurants, called *Taste of Scotland*. This guide, which appears annually, contains approximately 400 selected and tested eating places with details of location, approach, wheelchair access, smoking restrictions, opening times, specialities (including vegetarian dishes) and accommodation. If you want to be sure of finding well-prepared local cuisine, you may find it very useful *(see page 119)*.

Here we give a few recommendations listed according to the following price categories: **$$$** = expensive; **$$** = moderate; **$** = cheap.

Edinburgh

Channings, 12–16 South Learmonth Gardens, tel: 0131 315 2225. This takes a little finding but rewards the effort with superb service and a finely varied menu. **$$**.

Henderson's, 94 Hanover St, tel: 0131 225 2131. One of the oldest and best vegetarian restaurants in Britain. Closed Sunday except during Festival. **$**.

Howgate Restaurant, near Penicuik on the road to Peebles, tel: 01968 670000. Bistro-style meals served in ample quantities. **$$**.

Keepers, 138 Dundas St, tel: 0131 556 5707. If you like game, try here for traditional Scottish dishes. Closed Sunday and Monday. **$$**.

No 27 Charlotte Square, tel: 0131 243 9339. Within the headquarters of the National Trust for Scotland, this venue has rapidly grown popular for light dishes during the day and elegant dining at night. **$$**.

Tinelli, 139 Easter Road, tel: 0131 652 1932. Edinburgh has a long tradition of good Italian cuisine: this is one of the best. **$$**.

The Witchery, Castlehill, tel: 0131 225 5613. Scottish specialities and atmosphere appropriate to its name, situated directly below the Castle. **$$$**.

Glasgow

The Buttery, 652 Argyle St, tel: 0141 221 8188. Housed in an Anderston tenement, this is one of Glasgow's best-known restaurants; closed Sunday. **$$**.

Nairns, 13 Woodside Crescent, tel: 0141 353 0707. Run by chef Nick Nairn, with daily menu changes. **$$$**.

One Devonshire Gardens, tel: 0141 339 2001. The hotel known by its address has a restaurant with an excellent reputation – though its exclusive air may be a little off-putting. **$$$**.

The Puppet Theatre, 11 Ruthven Lane, tel: 0141 339 8444. Modern Scottish cooking at its best. Booking well ahead essential. Closed Monday. **$$**.

Stravaigin, 28 Gibson St, tel: 0141 334 2665. Offers pioneering dishes presented with flair. Food served till late in the café-bar. **$$**.

The Ubiquitous Chip, 12 Ashton Lane/Byres Rd, tel: 0141 334 5007. Glasgow institution with superb courtyard and highly-rated wine list. $$$.

Uplawmoor Hotel, Neilston Road, Uplawmoor, tel: 01505 850 565. An excellent reputation for quality bar meals plus a good à la carte menu in the restaurant. $.

Aberdeen and area

The Green Inn, 9 Victoria Road, Ballater, tel: 01339 755 701. Local Deeside produce used in imaginative ways; a former winner of the Taste of Scotland Restaurant of the Year. $$$.

The Lemon Tree, 5 West North St, tel: 01224 642 230. A restaurant by day, and a performing arts centre by night. $.

Silver Darlings, Pocra Quay, tel: 01224 576 229. High quality (and priced) fish dishes by the harbour. $$$.

Simpson's, 59 Queens Road, tel: 01224 327 777. A Spanish feel, but uses the best local produce. $$.

Argyll and the Islands

Loch Fyne Oyster Bar, Cairndow, tel: 01499 600 236. Ultra-fresh seafood served simply to maximise its flavour – and you can buy their produce to take home with you. $$.

The Tayvallich Inn, near Lochgilphead, tel: 01546 870 282, The spectacular outlook takes some beating, as does the seafood on the menu. A favourite with visiting yachtsmen. $$.

The Waterfront, The Pier, Oban, tel: 01631 563 110. Their motto is 'from the pier to the pan as fast as we can!' and, not unnaturally, seafood is the speciality. Open Easter to Christmas. $$$.

Central Scotland

Livingston's, 52 High St, Linlithgow, tel: 01506 846 565. Voted best out-of-town restaurant in 2000. It has charm, warmth and imaginative food. $$.

Quenelles, 4 Weir St, Falkirk, tel: 01324 877 411. Excellent Scottish produce in a family-run restaurant where nothing is too much trouble. $$.

Dundee and Angus

11 Park Avenue, Carnoustie, tel: 01241 853 336. A stunning eating experience – small and intimate and everything done with style. $$.

South Kingennie House, Kellas, Broughty Ferry, tel: 01382 350 562. The elegant dining room is matched by the quality of the food and the length of the wine list. $$.

Fife

Old Manor Hotel, Lundin Links, tel: 01333 320 368. Houses the Aithernie Restaurant, with imaginatively prepared and presented food. $$.

The Peat Inn, near Cupar, tel: 01334 840 206. World-class restaurant with only the finest ingredients and a magnificent wine list. Three AA rosettes. Closed Sunday and Monday. $$$.

The Seafood Restaurant, St Monan's, tel: 01333 730327. Plain name but far from plain menu, and has won several awards. Closed Monday during winter. $$.

The Woodside, High St, Aberdour, tel: 01383 860 328. Excellent value and choice in the dining room or bistro in this attractive Fife coastal town. $$.

Inverness and area

Café 1, 75 Castle Street, Inverness. Popular with local people; good value and pleasant bistro ambience. Closed Sunday. $$.

Made in Scotland, Station Road, Beauly, tel: 01463 782 578. Good value and child-friendly, it also has an excellent craft shop. $.

The Old Monastery, Drybridge, Buckie, tel: 01542 832 660. Classic dishes in modern style in lovely old building. Closed Monday. $$.

The Riverhouse, 1 Greig St, Inverness, tel: 01463 222 033. Fish, meat and game all feature on the menu, prepared in an open-plan kitchen where you can see the chefs at work. **$$$**.

Northern Highlands

The Portland Arms, Lybster, Caithness, tel: 01593 721 721. Bistro-style menu and formal dining room, both using local produce. **$$**.

The Royal Golf Hotel, Dornoch, tel: 01862 810 283. Meals served in a beautiful room overlooking the golf course and the Dornoch Firth, with local produce used as much as possible. Closed January and February. **$$**.

Orkney and Shetland

The Creel, St Margaret's Hope, South Ronaldsay, Orkney, tel: 01856 831 311. Rightly renowned for its seafood. Small and friendly, booking essential. Limited opening in winter. **$$**.

Monty's Bistro, 5 Mounthooly St, Lerwick, Shetland, tel: 01595 696 555. Good food, service and great atmosphere make for a fine eating experience. Closed Sunday and Monday. **$**.

Perthshire

The Bank, 32 High St, Crieff, tel: 01764 656 575. This place was once what its name implies, but now offers creative cooking. Closed Monday. **$$**.

Cargills, Lower Mill Street, Blairgowrie, tel: 01250 876 735. Popular bistro ideal for a relaxed meal followed by a stroll along the river. Closed Tuesday. **$$.**

Let's Eat, 77 Kinnoull St, Perth, tel: 01738 643 377; and **Let's Eat Again**, 33 George St, Perth, tel: 01738 633 771. Excellent bistro-style eating places, deservedly popular. Both **$$**.

The Loft, Golf Course Road, Blair Atholl, tel: 01796 481 377. Old beams and stone walls – but book early to avoid disappointment. **$$**.

Southern Scotland

Balcary Bay Hotel, Auchencairn, Castle Douglas, tel: 01556 640 217. Meals overlooking the sea and formal dinners in a magnificent setting. **$$$**.

Braidwoods, Drumastie Mill, Dalry, tel: 01294 833 544. Award-winning restaurant, does everything to highest standards. Menus changed daily. Closed Sunday pm to Tuesday pm. **$$$**.

Cellars, 149 Templehill, Troon, tel: 01292 317 448. Steeped in history with Art Deco interior. Dishes use the best local produce. Closed Tuesday. **$$**.

Cobbles, 7 Bowmont St, Kelso, tel: 01573 22 3548. Popular with locals and visitors. Good Scottish produce. **$**.

Fins, Fencefoot, Fairlie, tel: 01475 568 989. Excellent fish, traditional ingredients prepared in a modern style. **$$**.

Fouters Bistro, 24 Academy Street, Ayr, tel: 01292 261 391. Friendly atmosphere and modern Scottish dishes; this restaurant fully merits its two AA rosettes. Closed Sunday. **$$**.

West Highlands

Crannogs, Town Pier, Fort William. A converted bait store, now a very successful seafood restaurant. **$**.

The Fish Market, Station Road, Mallaig, tel: 01687 462 299. Specialises in seafood, and also renowned for its baking. **$$**.

The Green Welly Shop, Tyndrum, tel: 01838 400 271. A roadside stop that is hard to beat. Self-service but consistently high quality, and with a surprisingly varied menu. **$**.

The Old Pines, Spean Bridge, tel: 01397 712 324. All local ingredients prepared with care and skill, backed up with a well chosen wine list. **$$**.

Western Isles

The Stepping Stone, Balivanich, Benbecula. Offers everything from filled rolls to superb full meals using local produce. **$–$$$**.

ACTIVE HOLIDAYS

Scotland is a country for walkers (and fit, healthy cyclists). The Tourist Information Centres provide maps and descriptions of numerous cycle tours and walks. For a walk in the wind and rain in April or on a light evening after a long sunny day in September, it is hard to beat the mile-long, sandy beaches in Wester Ross or the Outer Hebrides, which are often completely deserted.

HIKING

The more energetic can join the 'Munro baggers' – those whose sole aim is to climb all 284 Scottish mountains over 3,000ft (914m). These peaks are named after Sir Hugh Munro who catalogued them in his 30-volume 'Munro Tables' at the end of the 19th century. The first man to achieve this feat was one Archibald Eneas Robertson, and until the 1970s only around a hundred people had managed to follow all the way in his footsteps. But it has now become a duty for record-hunters (the long-distance runner Mark Elsegood managed them all in only 66 days). Normal mortals are advised to take it more slowly.

The famous golf course
at St Andrews

These mountains are not high by alpine standards, with the highest, Ben Nevis, reaching only 4,406 ft (1,343 m). They are nevertheless challenging, bearing in mind that some must be climbed from sea level and that the sudden changes in the weather can endanger even the most experienced of climbers. But this is precisely the attraction of conquering peaks such as An Teallach or Sgurr Alasdair: Munro baggers are not exerting themselves just for the breathtaking view.

Perhaps the finest expedition on the Scottish hills is a complete traverse of the Cuillin Ridge in Skye. Taking in 11 Munros along the way, this walk, scramble and climb involves over 3,000 metres of ascent over the only peaks in the British Isles that require rock climbing equipment to get to their summits – for experienced walkers and climbers only.

SKIING

The idea of skiing in a romantic landscape has been sold successfully enough to give Scotland a winter tourist season. With five centres, each with 15 to 30 marked slopes and between six and 26 lifts, the central Highlands are the winter sports centre of Britain. Glencoe has interesting runs and a magnificent view, Glenshee and Cairngorm are the largest and most developed areas.

Skiing in Scotland does however have certain disadvantages: rapid changes in the weather coming from the Atlantic mean that the snow conditions are not very stable, and on top of this almost impossible to predict. The increasing devastation of the landscape is also cause for great concern: the slopes of Cairn Gorm are being severely eroded, as is all too evident once the snow melts.

GOLF

Those whose walking is limited to the golf course will find that golf is a cheap popular sport in Scotland – unless you insist on playing one of the famous courses: St Andrews, Troon or Carnoustie. Golfing enthusiasts should instead try Nairn, Machrihanish or even Royal Dornoch. In the south, in the Lowlands and on the east coast, golf courses are so thick on the ground that being unable to choose between them is the only thing that will stop you from playing. The Scottish Tourist Board's *Scotland Activity Holidays* brochure

Cycling

Cyclists do not have an easy time of it in Scotland because there are so many hills, but there are other compensations. Away from the main highways, there are numerous narrow roads with surprisingly good surfaces. Recent years have seen the development of a number of excellent cycle trails. These trails use dedicated cycle paths separated from other traffic.

Information about these routes, cycle hire, train connections within Scotland and ferries and flights to the islands, etc. can be obtained from the central information service of the Scottish Tourist Board, tel: 0131 332 2433.

alone lists nearly 300 places where golf can be played, some of which have several courses (the details provided include addresses, telephone numbers, prices, admission restrictions, etc).

SURFING

Surfing and windsurfing are becoming increasingly popular, which is scarcely surprising given Scotland's superb beaches, and good instruction for beginners is often available. For information contact the Scottish Windsurfing Association, c/o RYA Scotland, Caledonia House, South Gyle, Edinburgh, tel. 0131 317 7217. For seasoned surfers, the Hebridean island of Tiree, west of Mull, though not very easy to get to, has the most hours of sun in Scotland and extremely demanding wind conditions.

SAILING

In Scotland there is a more unusual way of exploring the country – by sea. Boat trips through the magnificent island world off the west coast are always to be recommended, but those who want to take the helm themselves should request information about boat hire, sailing courses, legal requirements, etc. from the Royal Yachting Association Scotland, Caledonia House, South Gyle, Edinburgh, tel. 0131 317 7388.

MUSEUMS AND ATTRACTIONS

Unless otherwise stated, all the museums mentioned in the 'Places' section of the guide are open from Monday to Saturday, from 10am at the latest and closing at the earliest at 5pm; on Sundays, museums open only in the afternoon, usually from 2pm. Some only open during the summer season, when opening times are in general longer (the Tourist Information Centres provide leaflets containing the exact times).

PRACTICAL INFORMATION

Getting There

BY AIR

British Airways flies every hour from Heathrow to both Edinburgh and Glasgow, and there are also regular British Airways flights from Manchester and Birmingham. From Heathrow and several English regional airports, Edinburgh and Glasgow are also served by British Midland and Air UK; Aberdeen is served by Brit Air and Air UK and Inverness is served by British Airways.

Continental Airlines fly direct from Glasgow to New York. Other transatlantic routes are via Iceland (Icelandair), Toronto (Air Canada, Canada 3000) or London (British Airways, American Airlines). In addition to low-cost, no-frills airlines such as Ryanair, Go and easyJet, there are also summer charter flights

Edinburgh airport (tel: 0131 333 1000) is 6 miles (10km) west of the city centre, with good road access and a useful airlink bus service to the heart of town. Glasgow airport (tel: 0141 887 1111) is 8 miles (13km) west of the city centre alongside the A8 motorway at junction 28. A coach service runs between the airport and Anderston and Buchanan bus stations in the heart of the city.

In Scotland, BA Express, otherwise known as Loganair, operates regular services between Glasgow and the Western Isles (Benbecula, Barra and Lewis); it is also possible to fly to Benbecula and Lewis from Inverness.

BY RAIL

There are regular train services from London Euston and Kings Cross operated by Virgin Trains and Great North Eastern Railways. For details and reservations tel: 03457 484950, or from outside the UK tel: 0133 238 7601. A Scot Rail sleeper service operates from Euston to Edinburgh, Fort William or Inverness (not Sat pm).

BY BUS

The cheapest form of public transport to Scotland is the long-distance bus, using the National Express service from England or Scottish Citylink (which, for example, runs buses three to five times daily from London to Edinburgh or Glasgow, a journey of 8–9 hours).

National Express: for journeys to Edinburgh, Glasgow, or indeed anywhere else in Scotland, tel: 0870 5808080.

Scottish Citylink: tel: 0990 505050.

BY CAR

Scotland is easily reached by car from major centres in England. From London, travellers can take the M40 motorway to Birmingham, the M6 to Carlisle and then on to Glasgow and destinations in the west of Scotland. For Edinburgh and the east, the A1, which is partly motorway, is the fastest route north, crossing the border near Berwick-upon-Tweed.

Getting Around

BY ROAD

The most important thing for visitors from outside Britain to remember when travelling in Scotland, or the rest of the United Kingdom, is that the British drive on the left.

Speed limits are 30 mph (48 km/h) in built-up areas, 60 mph (96 km/h) on ordinary roads and 70 mph (113 km/h) on motorways or dual carriageways. There are a few other points to note. Traffic already on a roundabout has right of way (and there are many junctions with roundabouts). The many single-lane roads with passing places, especially in the Highlands, are a delight, although their use requires a certain amount of caution (let the locals overtake). Stray sheep tend to cross the road just when one of the few cars you will meet on your journey is passing. But that is the only real hazard – Scotland's roads are relatively safe.

Hire cars are not cheap, but can be obtained at airports and in the larger towns from the usual companies. The requirements are a minimum age of 21, a driving licence and a credit card.

Hertz: in Edinburgh: tel: 0131 556 8311; Edinburgh airport: tel: 0131 333 1019; in Glasgow: tel: 0141 248 7736; Glasgow airport: 0141 887 2451.

Avis: in Edinburgh: tel: 0131 337 6363; Edinburgh airport: tel: 0131 333 1866.; Glasgow: tel: 0141 221 2827; Glasgow airport: 0141 887 2261.

Both the Automobile Association (AA) and the Royal Automobile Club (RAC) have reciprocal arrangements with North American motoring associations. For emergency assistance there are clearly marked telephones at the roadside, and members who need help should have the name of their organisation and their membership number ready when they ring.

BY BUS

All major towns and cities, and many smaller places, are linked by good bus services (though there are fewer on Sundays). Local enquiry at tourist information centres will produce timetables.

CITY TRANSPORT

The bus is the main form of transport in Edinburgh. In Glasgow there is an underground railway, which runs round the periphery of the city centre, as well

as orange city buses. A special bus line connects Glasgow's two main stations, Central Station (for England and the Southeast/shuttle to the ferry to Ireland in Stranraer) and Queen Street Station (the North/the Highlands, the East/Edinburgh). More detailed information can be obtained from the St Enoch Square Travel Centre.

> **Scenic railways**
> Scotland has some spectacular railway routes (for instance, the West Highland Line from Glasgow via Fort William to Mallaig), but only one that goes to the far north: from Inverness, branching off after Halkirk to Wick or Thurso.

BY FERRY

Caledonian MacBrayne has a near monopoly on west coast routes. Its 30 vessels link 23 islands to the mainland and each other via 52 ports. They sell hopscotch tickets and, best value for visitors with cars, rover tickets for driver and one passenger giving 8 or 15 days unlimited travel on most routes. Boats vary from the large, well-equipped car ferries operating to the Outer Hebrides to smaller vessels with wooden seats. For further information, contact: Caledonian MacBrayne, Ferry Terminal, Gourock, PA19 1QP, tel: 01475 650100; reservations tel: 0990 650000.

Facts for the Visitor

TRAVEL DOCUMENTS

The same entry regulations apply for Scotland as in the rest of the United Kingdom. Visitors from North America, Japan, most Commonwealth countries and EU countries do not need a visa for short stays. Check with the British Embassy in your home country if in doubt.

TOURIST INFORMATION

For visitors from North America, information about Scotland is available through the **British Tourist Authority**.

In Canada

111 Avenue Road, Suite 450, Toronto, Ontario M5R 3J8, tel: 416 925 6326.

In the US

625 N Michigan Avenue, Suite1510, Chicago, Illinois, 60611, tel: 1-800 462 2748.

7th Floor, 551 Fifth Avenue, New York, NY 10176, tel: 1-800 441 2748 or 212 986 2200. They also have a fax vault: 818 41 8265 (access via handset of fax machine only).

In the UK, visitors can write to the **Scottish Tourist Board** for information at 23 Ravelston Terrace, Edinburgh EH4 3EU, tel: 0131 332 2433, or visit the STB website at www.visitscotland.com

There is also an STB information centre at 9 Cockspur Street, London SW1E 5BL, tel: 0207 930 8661.

There is a network of Tourist Information Centres (TICs) across Scotland, and a selection is listed below, together with websites for Area Tourist Boards.

Edinburgh and Lothian

Edinburgh and Scotland Information Centre, 3 Princes Street, Edinburgh EH2 2QP (Waverley Market, at the main railway station), tel: 0131 473 3800, fax: 0131 473 3881, www.edinburgh.org

Edinburgh Airport Information Desk, tel: 0131 333 2167.

Glasgow and Clyde Valley

Main TIC: 11 George Square, Glasgow G2 1DY (opposite Queen Street Station), tel: 0141 204 4400, fax: 0141 204 4772, www.seeglasgow.com

Glasgow Airport Information Desk, tel: 0141 848 4440. Lanark, tel: 01555 661661.

Aberdeen and Grampian

Main TIC: St Nicholas House, Broad Street, Aberdeen AB19 1DE, tel: 01224 632727, fax: 01224 620415, www.agtb.org

Other TICs: Ballater (Easter–Oct), tel: 01339 755306. Braemar (Easter–Oct), tel: 01339 741600. Elgin, tel: 01343 542666.

Argyll, the Isles, Loch Lomond and the Trossachs

Website: www.visitscottish.heartlands.org Main TICs: Callander, tel: 01877 330342. Falkirk, tel: 01324 620244. Oban, tel: 01631 563122. Stirling, tel: 01786 475019. Tobermory, Mull (Apr–Oct), tel: 01688 302182.

Dundee and Angus

Website: www.angusanddundee.co.uk Main TIC: Dundee, tel: 01382 527527.

Fife

Website: www.standrews.com Main TICs: Dunfermline (Apr–Oct), tel: 01383 720999. St Andrews, tel: 01334 472021.

Highlands and Skye

Website: www.highlandfreedom.com Main TICs: Aviemore, tel: 01479 810363. Fort William, tel: 01397 703781. Inverness, tel: 01463 234353. Portree, Skye, tel: 01478 612137. Wick, tel: 01955 602596.

The Islands

Websites: www.witb.co.uk/www.visitorkney.com/www.shetland-tourism.co.uk Main TICs: Kirkwall, Orkney, tel: 01856 872856. Lerwick, Shetland, tel: 01595 693434. Stornoway, Lewis, tel: 01851 703088.

Perthshire
Website: www.perthshire.co.uk Main TICs: Dunkeld, tel: 01350 727688. Perth, tel: 01738 450600. Pitlochry, tel: 01796 472215.

Southern Scotland
Websites: www.ayrshire-arran.com/www.dumfriesandgalloway.co.uk/www.scot-borders.co.uk Main TICs: Ayr, tel: 01292 288688. Brodick, Arran, tel: 01770

CURRENCY
The monetary unit is the pound sterling, as in the rest of Great Britain: £1 = 100 pence. In addition to the Bank of England notes and coins, notes issued by the Bank of Scotland and Royal Bank of Scotland are also in circulation (same value and size, different designs), in denominations of £1, £5, £10, £20, £50 and £100 notes, and 1, 2, 5, 10, 20, 50 pence and £1 and £2 coins. Scottish bank notes are legal tender throughout Britain, but you may have difficulty changing them elsewhere.

The usual credit cards are taken by most hotels, restaurants, shops and petrol stations, etc. (the relevant signs are displayed on the doors).

*Tourist shops abound
in Edinburgh*

TIPPING
Taxi drivers expect about 10–15 percent of the fare. Waiters in restaurants should also be given 10–15 percent of the bill, if it is stated on the menu that service is not included (otherwise it is left to the discretion of the customer to show appreciation of good service). Bar staff in pubs etc. are not usually tipped. Tip porters and page boys at least £1. For good service in a country house hotel, leave something for the staff when you pay at reception. Scotland is not in general a country where a lot of tipping is expected.

OPENING TIMES
Shops
As in the rest of Britain, most shops open from 9.00am–5.30pm. Supermarkets often stay open much later. Some shops, particularly in smaller towns and villages, close on Saturday afternoon, and some have a mid-week half-day closure. Very few close at lunchtime. You will find many shops open on Sunday in most areas. Some petrol stations have useful small shops.
Banks
Monday to Friday 9.30am–3.30pm. Some in the larger towns and cities are open longer. In rural areas there are travelling banks serving even small villages.

SHOPPING AND SOUVENIRS

Edinburgh

Exclusive and unusual shops are to be found in the area between Princes Street and George Street; on Princes Street you will find not only numerous tartan, tweed and wool shops, but also **Jenners**, generally known as the 'Harrods of Edinburgh'; gift articles, souvenirs and 'Scottish specialities' are available in abundance along the Royal Mile, while in and around St Stephen Street and North West Circus Place there is a concentration of antique and second-hand shops.

> **Public Holidays**
> New Year's Day, 2 January, Good Friday, the first Monday in May, the last Monday in May, the first Monday in August, and 25 and 26 December.

Glasgow

Glasgow's markets are justifiably famous and not to be missed. Try the **Fishmarket** in Clyde Street, and the famous **Barras** fleamarket in Gallowgate to the east.

For more local colour there is **Paddy's Market** situated in the lanes between Clyde Street and Briggait. **Argyll Street**, **Sauchiehall Street** and the more upmarket **Buchanan Street** are Glasgow's great shopping thoroughfares. They are supplemented by a number of new shopping malls, including the impressive **Princes Square** and **Buchanan Galleries**, both in Buchanan Street.

Aberdeen

Everything you need (and much that you do not) can be found in the **Bon Accord Centre** and **St Nicholas Centre** in the inner city; in George Street north of the Bon Accord Centre there are some interesting second-hand and antique shops.

POSTAL SERVICES

Post offices are usually open from Monday to Friday from 9am to 5.30pm, Saturday often only till 1pm. The sub-post offices, i.e. postal counters in village shops, usually close at midday and/or one afternoon in the week.

TELEPHONES

Telephones accept 10, 20 and 50 pence pieces, also pound coins, and the minimum amount is 20p. There are card phones almost everywhere which also accept credit cards: cards ranging from £2 to £20 are obtainable from shops displaying the green and white Phonecard sign. Long-distance and international calls can be made from all public telephone boxes, with cheap rates from 6pm to 8am on weekdays, and all day on Sunday and public holidays. To call the US and Canada, dial 001 followed by the code and number. National inquiries, tel: 192, international inquiries, tel: 153.

DISABLED TRAVELLERS

The Scottish Council on Disability (Disability Scotland) will answer all relevant inquiries. A detailed list of hotels, bed and breakfasts, camp sites, sports centres, etc. with facilities for the disabled may be obtained from Disability Scotland, Princes House, 5 Shandwick Place, Edinburgh EH2 4RG, tel: 0131 229 8632, fax: 229 5168.

NEWSPAPERS

The Scotsman and the Sunday paper *Scotland on Sunday* have detailed reports on Scottish affairs as well as international news (the latter also has good restaurant tips and travel and culture articles). Scotland also has the popular newpapers *Daily Record*, *The Herald, Sunday Post* and *Sunday Mail*, and in most parts of the country all the English daily papers are available.

RADIO AND TELEVISION

Five television channels broadcast throughout the country: BBC1, BBC2, ITV (or the associated regional channels), Channel 4 and Channel 5. Details of the programmes are given in the daily press and in a number of broadcasting magazines, of which *Radio Times* and *TV Times* are the most widely circulated. The BBC has five national radio stations, and there are also regional BBC stations and numerous commercial radio stations.

Emergencies
The emergency number throughout Britain is 999. When you dial it (the calls are free) you will be asked whether you want the police, fire service or an ambulance, and possibly also the coastguard or mountain and cave rescue service. Have the number that you are calling from ready, and the address or location where help is needed.

CLOTHING

You should take waterproofs and warm clothing whenever you go to Scotland. If you are planning to do any serious walking, then sturdy footwear is necessary. It is not essential to dress up for concerts or the theatre, but some more expensive restaurants expect men to wear jackets and ties and women skirts or dresses for dinner.

TIME

In winter Great Britain is on Greenwich Mean Time (GMT), one hour earlier than Central European Time. In March the clocks are put forward one hour; at the end of October they are put back an hour.

ELECTRICITY

Electricity is 240V/50 Hz AC. Equipment designed for 220V AC can be used with an adapter.

HEALTH CARE

Visitors from other parts of Britain are, of course, entitled to free treatment under the National Health Service. For visitors from abroad, emergency treatment is free under the National Health Service, but other treatment must be paid for.

Citizens of EU countries benefit from a reciprocal health-care agreement with Britain. However, it is always wise to have good private health insurance cover. National Health Service prescription charges are high – approximately £6 per item – and many medicines are cheaper when bought over the counter from the pharmacist.

INSECTS

By far the most annoying thing you will encounter in Scotland is the midge. This biting little insect can be encountered just about anywhere in the Highlands from June to September, and particularly in the warm, humid conditions on the islands and along the west coast. This tiny creature can make your life a misery, so if you are heading outdoors, take some repellent.

FURTHER LEARNING

For those interested in learning more about Scottish culture, there are Gaelic courses and instruction in every kind of traditional craft in the Sabhal Mor Ostaig Gaelic School, An Teanga, Isle of Skye, tel. 01471 844373.

DIPLOMATIC REPRESENTATION

American Consulate General: 3 Regent Terrace, Edinburgh EH7, tel: 0131 556 8315.
Australian High Commission: Australia House, Strand, London WC2B 4LA, tel: 0171 379 4334..
Canadian High Commission: Macdonald House, 1 Grosvenor Square, London W1, tel: 0171 258 6600.

ACCOMMODATION

Scotland is made for the independent traveller, with lodgings from the prohibitively expensive to simple bed and breakfast accommodation, camp sites and youth hostels. Scotland is well provided with camp sites, especially on the southern coasts, and of course at all the tourist spots, but there are two substantial problems with camping in Scotland: the weather (all year – wet in the summer and cold in the winter) and the midges (in season). Holiday cottages and flats are also a popular alternative for all those who have decided beforehand where they want to spend their holiday.

A complete list of Scottish TICs and brochures on all types of accommodation can be obtained from the central information service of the Scottish Tourist Board, tel: 0131 332 2433 (www.visitscotland.com). The Scottish Youth Hostel Association (7 Glebe Crescent, Stirling FK8 2JA, tel: 01786 891400, fax: 891333, e-mail: info@syha.org.uk) also publishes a list of its hostels.

Cheap accommodation outside term time, which is available to everyone, not just to students, is provided by the universities of Edinburgh, Glasgow, Dundee, St Andrews, Stirling and Strathclyde. For information, contact the BUAC (British Universities Accommodation Consortium Limited), Box H97 University Park, Nottingham, NG7 2RD, tel: 0115 950 4571, fax: 942 2505.

Outside the busy summer season, it is quite possible to explore Scotland without planning everything in advance. The Tourist Information Centres are very helpful, and useful sources of local information.

The following are suggestions for destinations that appear in the guide, arranged according to price: $$$ = expensive; $$ = moderate; $ = cheap.

Edinburgh

The Bonham, 35 Drumsheugh Gardens, tel: 0131 623 9319, e-mail: reserve@thebonham.com A seriously trendy designer interior in a fine Victorian building, with a superb restaurant. $$$.

Borthwick Castle, North Middleton, near Dalkeith, tel: 01875 820 514. A real castle with every comfort (at a price) about 15 miles/25km south of the city centre. $$$.

The Caledonian, Princes Street, tel: 0131 459 9988, e-mail: ednchhirm@hilton.com Centrally situated and elegantly furnished. $$$.

Sibbet House, 26–8 Northumberland St, tel: 0131 556 1078. Created from two fine houses in the New Town; reasonably priced for what it offers. $$.

SYHA, 18 Eglinton Crescent, tel: 0131 337 1120, e-mail: info@syha.org.uk A magnificent piece of architecture, and friendly to boot. $.

Glasgow

Babbity Bowster, 16–18 Blackfriars St, tel: 0141 552 5055, e-mail: babbity bowster@gofornet.co.uk A lively bar with rooms in the heart of the Merchant City, named after a Scottish folk dance. $$.

Gleddoch House, Langbank, 30 miles/48km west of Glasgow tel: 01475 540 711, e-mail: gleddochhouse @ukonline.co.uk A luxurious country house with fine Scottish cuisine and a golf course. $$$.

The Inn on the Green, 25 Greenhead St, tel: 0141 554 0165, e-mail: sales@theinnonthegreen.co.uk Next to Glasgow Green and the River Clyde. $$.

One Devonshire Gardens, in the West End, tel: 0141 339 2001, e-mail: onedevonshire@btconnect.com A very smart hotel with a superb restaurant. $$$.

The University of Strathclyde Residence Services, 50 Richmond St, tel: 0141 553 4148, e-mail: rescat@mis.strath.ac.uk A range of affordable accommodation in the student halls of residence during University holiday periods. $.

Aberdeen and area
Ardoe House, South Deeside Road, Aberdeen, tel: 01224 860 660, e-mail: ardoe@macdonald-hotels.co.uk This is a classic Scots baronial mansion with full leisure facilities. $$.

Craiglynn Hotel, 36 Fonthill Road, Aberdeen, tel: 01224 584 050, e-mail: info@craiglynn.co.uk Victorian elegance and Scottish cuisine. $$$.

Raemoir House, Banchory, tel: 01330 824 884, e-mail: raemoirhse@aol.com A baronial manor set in 3,500 acres (1,415 hectares) of woodland. $$.

Argyll and the Islands
Apple Lodge, Lochranza, Isle of Arran, tel: 01770 830 229, e-mail: applelodge@easicom.com Set in its own grounds not far from Lochranza Castle. $.

Assapol House, Bunessan, Isle of Mull, tel: 01681 700 258, e-mail: alex@assapol.com A real haven of tranquillity on the beautiful island of Mull. $$.

Dungallan House, Gallanach Road, Oban, tel: 01631 563 799, e-mail: welcome@dungallanhotel-oban.co.uk Beautifully sited on Oban Bay and renowned for its seafood. $$.

Royal Hotel, Tighnabruaich, tel: 01700 811 239, e-mail: royalhotel@btinternet.com Very well appointed rooms and a superb restaurant; understandably popular with visiting yachtsmen and women. $$.

Central Scotland
Inverbeg Inn, Luss, Loch Lomond, tel: 01436 860 679. An old coaching inn with superb views across the loch. $$.

Roman Camp Hotel, Callander, tel: 01877 330 003, e-mail: mail@roman-camp-hotel.co.uk A peaceful situation in this busy tourist town. $$.

The Topps, Fintry Rd, Denny, tel: 01324 822 471, e-mail: jennifer@thetopps.f9.co.uk A comfortable guest house with a highly-rated restaurant. $.

Dundee and Angus
Park Hotel, John St, Montrose, tel: 01674 663 400, e-mail: recep@montrosepark.co.uk Offers a friendly welcome and excellent food. $$.

A dramatic backdrop to Loch Lomond

Queens Hotel, 160 Nethergate, Dundee, tel: 01382 322 515. Dundee's oldest and grandest hotel, completely refurbished. **$$**.

Woodlands Hotel, Panmure Terrace, Barnhill, Dundee, tel: 01382 480 033. Set in 4 acres (1.5 hectares) of grounds near Broughty Ferry. **$$**.

Fife

Balbirnie House, Markinch, tel: 01592 610 066, e-mail: balbirnie@ btinternet.com Maintains the highest standards throughout. **$$$**.

Balcomie Links Hotel, Crail, tel: 01333 450 237. Close to the harbour in this pretty village, with golf courses nearby. **$$**.

Rufflets, Strathkinness Low Rd, St Andrews, tel: 01334 472 594, e-mail: reservations@rufflets.co.uk A country house hotel in the golf resort and university town. **$$$**.

Sandford Country House, Newton Hill, Wormit. In a peaceful setting on the south side of the Tay. **$$**.

Inverness and area, and Strathspey

Boat Hotel, Boat of Garten, tel: 01479 831 258, e-mail: holidays@boathotel. co.uk Convenient for the bird reserve at Loch Garten; offers a genuine welcome. **$$**.

Bunchrew House, Bunchrew, Inverness, tel: 01463 234 917, e-mail: welcome@bunchrew-inverness.co.uk Beautifully sited overlooking the sea. **$$**.

Cairngorm Hotel, Grampian Road, Aviemore, tel: 01479 810 233. Friendly service at an affordable price. **$$**.

Dunain Park Hotel, Inverness, tel: 01463 230 512, e-mail: dunainpark hotel@btinternet.com Offers fine Scottish cuisine and has a sauna and swimming pool. **$$$**.

Glenmorangie House, Cadboll, Fearn, tel: 01862 871 671, e-mail: relax@glenmorangieplc.co.uk Offers the ultimate in hospitality in a beautiful area. **$$**.

Golf Hotel, Seabank Road, Nairn, tel: 01667 452 301, e-mail: rooms@ morton-hotels.com Within an hour's drive of 25 golf courses, and has a pool and gym. **$$**.

The Osprey Hotel, Ruthven Road, Kingussie, tel: 01540 661 510, e-mail: aileen@ospreyhotel.co.uk Provides a high standard of hospitality with food to match. **$**.

Northern Highlands

Altnaharra Hotel, Bettyhill, tel: 01549 411 222. In a superb location near Loch Naver. **$$**.

Dornoch Castle Hotel, Castle St, Dornoch, tel: 01862 810 216. Close to the golf course and cathedral. **$$**.

Summer Isles Hotel, Achiltibuie, tel: 01854 622 282, e-mail: summerisles hotel@aol.com A superb outlook and a restaurant with food to match the view. **$$**.

Orkney and Shetland

Ayre Hotel, Harbour Front, Kirkwall, Orkney, tel: 01856 873 001. A good central base. **$$**.

Burrastow House, Walls, Shetland, tel: 01595 809 307, e-mail: burr. hs.hotel@zetnet.co.uk Worth all the effort of getting there for its atmosphere and superb food. Closed January to March. **$$**.

Foveran Hotel, St Ola, Kirkwall, Orkney, tel: 01856 872 389, e-mail: foveranhotel@aol.com Offers the genuine Orcadian experience in comfortable surroundings. **$$**.

Perthshire

Auchterarder House, Auchterarder, tel: 01764 663 646, e-mail: auchterarder @wrensgroup.com One of Scotland's finest country house hotels, in 17 acres (7 hectares) of beautiful grounds. **$$$**.

Green Park Hotel, Clunie Bridge Rd, Pitlochry, tel: 01796 473 248, e-mail: bookings@thegreenpark.co.uk Overlooks Loch Faskally. **$$**.

Huntingtower Hotel, Crieff Road, Perth, tel: 01738 583 771, e-mail: reception.huntingtower@talk21.com An Edwardian mansion west of Perth with two restaurants. **$$**.

Parklands Hotel, 2 St Leonards Bank, Perth, tel: 01738 622 451, e-mail: parklands.perth@virgin.net A beautifully decorated classical town house. **$$**.

Southern Scotland

Cosses, Ballantrae, tel: 01465 831 363, e-mail: cosses@compuserve.com Small but superbly run, with all food, even the bread, home-made. Closed December and January. **$$**.

Dunlaverock Country House, Coldingham, Berwickshire, tel: 01890 771 450, e-mail: dunlaverock@lineone.net Beautifully set on the east coast. **$$**.

The Ley, Innerleithen, tel: 01896 830240. An award-winning guesthouse in attractive countryside. **$$**.

Mansfield House, Weensland Rd, Hawick, tel: 01450 360 400, e-mail: ian@mansfield-house.com A Fine Victorian mansion in the heart of the Borders. **$$**.

Priory House, Broomfields, Largs, tel: 01475 686 460. In two 19th century buildings on the Promenade. **$$**.

The Roxburghe, Heiton, Kelso, tel: 01573 450 331, e-mail: hotel@roxburghe.net Has four-poster beds and a championship golf course. **$$$**.

Savoy Park Hotel, 16 Racecourse Road, Ayr, tel: 01292 266 112, e-mail: mail@savoypark.com Family-run, and offers excellent value. **$$**.

Station Hotel, Dumfries. A plain, reasonably priced hotel, good for an overnight stay and decent meal. **$**.

Opposite: an Inverewe hotel

West Highlands and Skye

Allt-nan-Ros Hotel, Onich, tel: 01855 821 210, email: allt-nan-ros@zetnet.co.uk A 19th century shooting lodge on Loch Leven. **$$**.

Cuillin Hills Hotel, Portree, Isle of Skye, tel: 01478 612 003, e-mail: office@cuillinhills.demon.co.uk Overlooks Portree Bay. **$$**.

Flodigarry Country House Hotel, Staffin, Isle of Skye, tel: 01470 552 203. Hotel set in a historic mansion with stunning sea and mountain views. **$$**.

Glen Loy Lodge, near Fort William, tel: 01397 712 700, e-mail: glenloy.lodge@virgin.net A charming country house decorated and furnished in 1920s style. **$$**.

Kinloch Lodge, Sleat, Isle of Skye, tel: 01471 833 214, e-mail: kinloch@dial.pipex.com The home of Lord and Lady Macdonald; offers every comfort, with superb cooking. **$$**.

The Moorings Hotel, Banavie, Fort William, tel: 01397 772 797, e-mail: moorings@lochaberhotels.freeserve.co.uk A coaching inn with a great view of Ben Nevis. **$$**.

The Plockton Hotel, Harbour St, Plockton, tel: 01599 544 274, e-mail: sales@plocktonhotel.co.uk In the centre of this picturesque lochside village. **$$**.

Western Isles

Caberfeidh Hotel, Manor Park, Stornoway, Isle of Lewis, tel: 01851 702 604, e-mail: caberfeidh@calahotels.com Set in its own grounds and offers all facilities. **$$**.

Isle of Barra Hotel, Tangasdale, Barra, tel: 01871 810 383. Idyllic, on a bay of white sand washed by the Atlantic. **$$**.

Scarista House, Isle of Harris, tel: 01859 550 238, e-mail: tnpmartin@ukgateway.net Picturesque hotel that specialises in using organic produce. **$$$**.

INDEX